Betty Crocker

the big book of chicken

Houghton Mifflin Harcourt
Boston • New York • 2015

GENERAL MILLS

Creative Content and Publishing Director:
Elizabeth Nientimp

Food Content Marketing Manager:
Heather Reid Liebo

Senior Editor: Grace Wells

Editor: Lori Fox

Kitchen Manager: Ann Stuart

Recipe Development and Testing:
Betty Crocker Kitchens

Photography: General Mills Photography
Studios and Image Library

HOUGHTON MIFFLIN HARCOURT

Publisher: Natalie Chapman

Editorial Director: Cindy Kitchel

Executive Editor: Anne Ficklen

Associate Editor: Heather Dabah

Managing Editor: Marina Padakis

Associate Production Editor:
Helen Seachrist

Cover Design: Tai Blanche

Interior Design and Layout: Tai Blanche

Production Coordinator: Kimberly Kiefer

Library of Congress Cataloging-in-Publication Data:

Crocker, Betty.

The big book of chicken / Betty Crocker.

pages cm

Includes index.

ISBN 978-0-544-45435-4 (trade paper); 978-0-544-45364-7 (ebk.)

1. Cooking (Chicken) I. Title. II. Title: Betty Crocker, the big book of chicken.

TX750.5.C45C7485 2015

641.6'65—dc23

2014033602

Manufactured in the United States of America

DOC 10 9 8 7 6 5 4 3 2 1

Cover photo: Top (left to right): Chicken and Dumplings (page 182); Caribbean Chicken Kabobs (page 22), Fried Chicken and Waffle Sandwich Bites (page 126); Cheese-Stuffed Buffalo Chicken Rolls (page 90)

Bottom (left to right): Crunchy Cornmeal Chicken with Mango-Peach Salsa (page 134); Moroccan Spatchcocked Chicken (page 64)

The Betty Crocker Kitchens seal guarantees success in your kitchen. Every recipe has been tested in America's Most Trusted Kitchens™ to meet our high standards of reliability, easy preparation and great taste.

FIND MORE GREAT IDEAS AT
BettyCrocker.com

Dear Friends,

Supper is calling and if you're like many others, you're standing in front of the fridge wondering what to make. The appeal of chicken, no matter who you talk to, results in conversation and descriptions that are entirely cliché such as "Chicken is so versatile and easy to fix that you can do just about anything with it and almost everyone loves it."

In this *Big Book of Chicken,* you'll want to check out the Chicken Primer at the beginning of the book for buying, storing and thawing information along with timetables for roasting, broiling and grilling. We've also included handy information on cooked chicken yields and substituting chicken pieces. And be sure to browse our special features offering quick recipe ideas for dry rubs and marinades, side dishes, chicken tenders and leftover cooked chicken.

Then, we've got you covered with great chicken creations for the grill, oven choices, easy skillet ideas plus one-pot and slow cooker favorites that will help you get dinner on the table with ease. From family dinners to backyard barbecues and casual entertaining, look no further.

How about exploring the exotic taste of Moroccan Spatchcocked Chicken or luscious Herb-Garlic Butter Spatchcocked Chicken? Never heard of this cooking method? Spatchcocking, with its whimsical name, is an older cooking term describing an easy method for butterflying a whole chicken so it opens up and flattens out like a book. The list of great-tasting chicken recipes you will find here goes on and on—are you getting your taste buds ready?

Look for these helpful icons:

* QUICK *   * CALORIE-CONTROLLED *

Happy Cooking!
Betty Crocker

contents

chicken primer

Chicken is like a blank culinary canvas. It can be served any way you like—in skillet sautés or slow cooker dishes, roasted or fried or in sandwiches or salads, just for a start—and it works with just about any flavoring. Explore global tastes like Thai, Moroccan, Mediterranean, Chinese, Indian, Caribbean, Mexican, Italian, French and classic American favorites—all right here. Before getting started stirring it up in the kitchen, check our helpful chicken know-how information below.

Buying Fresh Chicken

- Look for tightly wrapped packages without tears, holes or leaks and with little or no liquid.
- Check for a fresh odor; if it doesn't smell right, don't buy it.
- Choose cold packages, and stay away from those stacked above the top of the meat case—which may not be cold enough.
- Don't buy any packages if the sell-by date has already passed.
- Whole birds and cut-up pieces should be plump and meaty with smooth, moist-looking skin and no traces of feathers.
- Boneless skinless products should be plump and moist.

- Chicken skin color can vary from yellow to white and doesn't indicate quality.
- Cut ends of the bones should be pink to red in color.
- Place packages in plastic bags so juices don't drip on and contaminate other foods.
- Place chicken in the refrigerator as soon as you get home. If you're shopping on a hot day or you'll take longer than 30 minutes to get home, store it in an ice-packed cooler.

Storing Chicken

- Chicken packaged in clear, sealed plastic wrap on a plastic tray doesn't need to be repackaged.
- Chicken wrapped in butcher paper should be repackaged tightly in plastic wrap, foil or resealable food-storage plastic bags.
- Store chicken in the meat compartment or coldest part of your refrigerator, or freeze it as soon as possible.
- Cook or freeze chicken within 2 days of the sell-by date.
- If chicken was purchased frozen or was frozen at home, keep it in the refrigerator after thawing for the number of days listed in the Timetable for Storing Chicken, page 7. If it was refrigerated several days before freezing, use it the same day you thaw it.

TIMETABLE FOR THAWING CHICKEN

For food safety reasons, never thaw chicken at room temperature. Cook chicken the same day it's thawed. **Refrigerator Thawing:** Place chicken in a pan with sides or in a resealable food-storage plastic bag to catch drips. Allow about 24 hours for 3 to 4 pounds. **Cold-Water Thawing:** Submerge the packaged chicken in cold water, changing the water every 30 minutes. Allow 30 minutes per pound.

Type of Chicken	Weight	Refrigerator Thawing Time	Cold-Water Thawing Time
Chicken, Whole	3 to 4 pounds	1 day (24 hours)	1½ to 2 hours
Chicken, Parts	Up to 4 pounds	3 to 9 hours	1½ to 2 hours

TIMETABLE FOR STORING CHICKEN

Type of Chicken	Refrigerator (36°F to 40°F)	Freezer (0°F or colder)
Uncooked, whole or in parts	1 to 2 days	12 months (whole) 9 months (parts)
Uncooked Ground	1 to 2 days	3 to 4 months
Cooked	2 days	4 months

TIMETABLE FOR ROASTING CHICKEN

Roasting time is a general guideline.

Type of Chicken	Weight	Oven Temperature	Roasting Time
Whole Chicken (not stuffed)*	3 to 3½ pounds	375°F	1¾ to 2 hours

* For optimal food safety and even doneness, the USDA recommends cooking stuffing separately. However, if you choose to stuff the chicken, it's necessary to use an accurate food thermometer to make sure the center of the stuffing reaches a safe minimum temperature of 165°F. Cooking home-stuffed chicken is riskier than cooking those that are not stuffed. Even if the chicken itself has reached the safe minimum internal temperature of 165°F, the stuffing may not have reached the same. Bacteria can survive in stuffing that has not reached 165°F, possibly resulting in foodborne illness. Do not stuff chicken that will be grilled, smoked, fried or microwaved because it will never get hot enough in the center to be safe.

TIMETABLE FOR GRILLING CHICKEN

The times below are based on medium direct heat. Grill chicken until the internal temperature is at least 165°F, or until juice is clear when thickest part is cut; for whole chickens, take temperature in thigh, not touching bone. Turn chicken breasts once halfway through grilling. Turn chicken parts two to three times.

Cut of Chicken	Size	Grilling Time
Cut-Up Broiler-Fryer	3 to 3½ pounds	35 to 40 minutes
Bone-In Split Breasts (Breast Halves)	2½ to 3 pounds	20 to 25 minutes
Boneless Skinless Breasts	4 ounces each	15 to 20 minutes
Boneless Skinless Thighs	4 ounces each	20 to 24 minutes
Ground Chicken Patties	½ inch (4-inch diameter)	10 to 12 minutes

TIMETABLE FOR BROILING CHICKEN

Set the oven control to broil. Check the owner's manual for whether the door should be partially opened or closed during broiling. Place chicken on a rack in the broiler pan. Broil for the time listed, turning once, until a thermometer reaches at least 165°F or until the juice is clear when centers of thickest pieces are cut.

Cut of Chicken	Size	Broiling Time
Cut Up	3 to 3½ pounds	Skin side down 30 minutes; turn. Broil 15 to 25 minutes longer (7 to 9 inches from heat).
Bone-In Split Breasts	2½ to 3 pounds	25 to 35 minutes (7 to 9 inches from heat)
Boneless Skinless Breasts	4 ounces each	15 to 20 minutes (4 to 6 inches from heat)
Boneless Skinless Thighs	4 ounces each	10 to 12 minutes (4 to 6 inches from heat)
Wings	2 to 2½ pounds	10 minutes (5 to 7 inches from heat)

COOKED CHICKEN YIELDS

Remove the guesswork from deciding whether you will have enough cooked chicken for your favorite recipe by using this handy chart.

Type of Chicken	Weight	Yield of Chopped, Cubed or Shredded Cooked Chicken
Whole Chicken	3 to 3½ pounds	2½ to 3 cups
Bone-In Split Breasts	1½ pounds	2 cups
Boneless Skinless Breasts	1½ pounds	3 cups
Bone-In Thighs and Drumsticks	1½ pounds	1¾ cups

Substituting Chicken Pieces

You can substitute any chicken pieces for a cut-up chicken by using the same weight in breasts, thighs, legs or wings. If you use all breasts or thighs, which are thicker and meatier, you may need to increase cooking time.

Boning Chicken Breasts & Cutting Up a Whole Chicken How-tos

Cut-up chickens and boneless parts are readily available. If you want to do it yourself, or find a bargain on whole chickens, these are guides show you how.

Boning Chicken Breasts

Loosen keel bone and white cartilage by running tip of index finger around both sides. Pull out bone in one or two pieces.

Insert tip of knife under long rib bone. Resting knife against bones, use steady, even pressure to gradually trim meat away from bones. Cut rib cage away from breast, cutting through shoulder joint to remove entire rib cage. Repeat on other side.

Slip knife under white tendons on either side of breast; loosen and pull out tendons (grasp end of tendons with paper towel if tendons are slippery). Remove skin if desired. Cut breast lengthwise in half.

The Chicken Skin Myth

Cooking chicken with the skin on adds to the flavor, not the fat. Research has found that the fat doesn't soak into the meat during cooking. Leaving the skin on also helps keep juices in, creating meat that is more moist and tender. It's the skin itself that has the fat, calories and cholesterol, so discard it after cooking.

Cutting Up a Whole Chicken

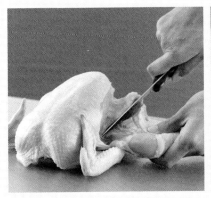

Cut off each leg by cutting skin between thigh and body; continue cutting through meat between tail and hip joint, cutting as closely as possible to backbone. Bend leg back until hip joint pops out as shown.

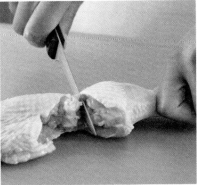

Separate thigh and drumstick by cutting about ⅛ inch from the fat line toward the drumstick as shown. (A thin white fat line runs crosswise at joint between drumstick and thigh.)

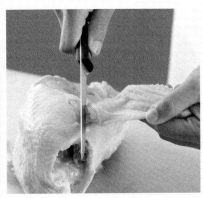

Remove each wing from body by cutting into wing joint with sharp knife, rolling knife to let the blade follow through at the curve of joint as shown.

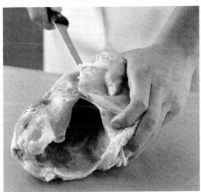

Separate back from breast by holding body, neck end down, and cutting downward along each side of backbone.

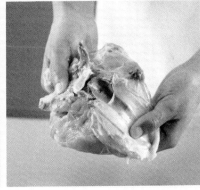

Bend breast halves back to pop out the keel bone. Remove keel bone as shown in Boning Chicken Breasts, left.

CHAPTER 1

On the Grill

buffalo–blue cheese chicken burgers

Prep Time: 35 Minutes • **Start to Finish:** 35 Minutes • 6 burgers

1¾ lb ground chicken

¼ cup Buffalo wing sauce

½ teaspoon salt

1 to 3 drops red pepper sauce

6 burger buns, split

6 leaves green leaf lettuce

¼ cup refrigerated chunky blue cheese dressing

¼ cup crumbled blue cheese (1 oz)

1 Heat gas or charcoal grill. In large bowl, mix chicken, Buffalo wing sauce, salt and red pepper sauce. Shape mixture into 6 patties, ½ inch thick.

2 Carefully brush oil on grill rack. Place patties on grill over medium heat. Cover grill; cook 10 to 12 minutes, turning once, until thermometer inserted in center of patties reads 165°F. During last 2 minutes of cooking, add buns, cut side down, to grill.

3 Place lettuce and burgers on bun bottoms. In small bowl, stir together dressing and blue cheese. Spoon mixture on burgers. Cover with bun tops.

1 Burger: Calories 330; Total Fat 17g (Saturated Fat 4.5g; Trans Fat 0g); Cholesterol 85mg; Sodium 890mg; Total Carbohydrate 23g (Dietary Fiber 1g); Protein 22g **Exchanges:** 1½ Starch, 2½ Medium-Fat Meat, ½ Fat **Carbohydrate Choices:** 1½

mexican chicken burgers

Prep Time: 35 Minutes • **Start to Finish:** 35 Minutes • 4 burgers

- 1 lb ground chicken
- 1 package (1 oz) taco seasoning mix
- 4 slices (1 oz each) Monterey Jack cheese
- 4 burger buns, split
- ¼ cup guacamole
- ¼ cup chunky-style salsa

1 Heat gas or charcoal grill. In large bowl, mix chicken and taco seasoning mix. Shape mixture into 4 patties, about ¾ inch thick.

2 Carefully brush oil on grill rack. Place patties on grill over medium heat. Cover grill; cook 14 to 16 minutes, turning once, until thermometer inserted in center of patties reads 165°F. During last 2 minutes of cooking, top each patty with cheese slice.

3 Place burgers on bun bottoms; top each with 1 tablespoon guacamole and 1 tablespoon salsa. Cover with bun tops.

1 Burger: Calories 400; Total Fat 18g (Saturated Fat 8g; Trans Fat 0.5g); Cholesterol 90mg; Sodium 1420mg; Total Carbohydrate 28g (Dietary Fiber 2g); Protein 32g **Exchanges:** 1 Starch, 1 Other Carbohydrate, 4 Lean Meat, 1 Fat **Carbohydrate Choices:** 2

swap it out

Ground turkey or lean ground beef can be used instead of the chicken for these south-of-the-border burgers.

grilled ranch chicken fillet sandwiches

Prep Time: 35 Minutes • **Start to Finish:** 1 Hour 35 Minutes • 4 sandwiches

½ cup ranch dressing

1 tablespoon chopped fresh chives

4 boneless skinless chicken breasts (about 1¼ lb)

4 slices Canadian bacon

4 whole-grain burger buns, split

2 tablespoons mayonnaise or salad dressing

2 tablespoons chopped fresh parsley

1 very large tomato, sliced

1 medium cucumber, thinly sliced

1 In shallow glass or plastic dish, mix ¼ cup of the dressing and the chives. Add chicken; turn to coat. Cover; refrigerate 1 to 2 hours, turning chicken occasionally.

2 Heat gas or charcoal grill. Place chicken on grill over medium heat. Cover grill; cook 15 to 20 minutes, turning once or twice, until juice of chicken is clear when center of thickest part is cut (at least 165°F). Add bacon to grill for last 2 to 3 minutes of cooking time to heat. If desired, add buns, cut side down, for last 4 minutes of grilling or until toasted.

3 In small bowl, mix remaining ¼ cup dressing, the mayonnaise and parsley; spread on cut sides of buns. Layer bacon, chicken, tomato and cucumber in each bun. Cover with bun tops.

1 Sandwich: Calories 530; Total Fat 29g (Saturated Fat 5g; Trans Fat 0.5g); Cholesterol 110mg; Sodium 890mg; Total Carbohydrate 24g (Dietary Fiber 4g); Protein 44g
Exchanges: 1½ Starch, 5½ Medium-Fat Meat **Carbohydrate Choices:** 1½

swap it out

Substitute any flavor creamy salad dressing instead of the ranch flavor if you prefer.

easy grilled chicken tacos

Prep Time: 15 Minutes • **Start to Finish:** 30 Minutes • 4 servings (2 tacos each)

1 tablespoon vegetable oil

1 tablespoon lime juice

1 tablespoon taco seasoning mix (from 1-oz package)

2 boneless skinless chicken breasts

1 can (15 oz) black beans, drained, rinsed

⅓ cup chunky-style salsa

2 tablespoons chopped fresh cilantro

8 flour tortillas for soft tacos and fajitas (6 inch)

1 Heat gas or charcoal grill. In gallon-size resealable food-storage plastic bag, mix oil, lime juice and taco seasoning mix until smooth. Add chicken; seal bag. Shake until chicken is evenly coated.

2 Place chicken on grill over medium heat. Cover grill; cook 12 to 15 minutes, turning once, until juice of chicken is clear when center of thickest part is cut (at least 165°F). Let stand 5 minutes.

3 Meanwhile, in 2-quart saucepan, heat beans, salsa and cilantro over medium heat, stirring occasionally, until hot. Remove from heat; cover and keep warm.

4 Cut chicken crosswise into strips. Divide chicken on half of each tortilla; top with bean mixture. Fold other half of tortilla over filling.

Broiling Directions: Set oven control to broil. Spray broiler rack with cooking spray. Place coated chicken on rack in broiler pan. Broil with tops about 4 inches from heat 6 to 9 minutes, turning after 5 minutes, until juice of chicken is clear when center of thickest part is cut (at least 165°F). Let stand 5 minutes. Continue as directed in step 3.

1 Serving: Calories 440; Total Fat 10g (Saturated Fat 2g; Trans Fat 1.5g); Cholesterol 35mg; Sodium 1110mg; Total Carbohydrate 60g (Dietary Fiber 13g); Protein 25g **Exchanges:** 4 Starch, ½ Vegetable, 1½ Lean Meat, ½ Fat **Carbohydrate Choices:** 4

chipotle grilled chicken salad

Prep Time: 30 Minutes • **Start to Finish:** 50 Minutes • 4 servings

4 boneless skinless chicken breasts (about 1¼ lb)

¾ cup bottled chipotle marinade

½ cup chunky-style salsa

¼ cup chopped fresh cilantro

2 tablespoons bottled chipotle marinade

2 tablespoons olive oil

Grated peel of 1 medium lime (2 teaspoons)

Juice of 1 medium lime (almost ⅓ cup)

4 cups torn romaine lettuce

1 cup frozen corn, cooked, cooled

½ cup chopped red bell pepper

1 can (15 oz) black beans, drained, rinsed

1 In large nonmetal dish or resealable food-storage plastic bag, place chicken and ¾ cup chipotle marinade; turn to coat. Cover dish or seal bag; refrigerate at least 20 minutes or up to 2 hours to marinate.

2 Heat gas or charcoal grill. Remove chicken from marinade; discard marinade. Place chicken on grill over medium heat. Cover grill; cook 10 to 12 minutes, turning halfway through grilling, until juice is clear when center of thickest part is cut (at least 165°F). Let stand 5 minutes; cut crosswise into ½-inch strips.

3 In small bowl, stir together salsa, cilantro, 2 tablespoons chipotle marinade, the oil, lime peel and lime juice. In large bowl, toss lettuce, corn, bell pepper and beans; toss with salsa mixture.

4 Divide bean mixture among 4 serving plates. Top each with chicken. If desired, serve with sour cream.

1 Serving: Calories 420; Total Fat 12g (Saturated Fat 2g; Trans Fat 0g); Cholesterol 75mg; Sodium 780mg; Total Carbohydrate 43g (Dietary Fiber 12g); Protein 36g **Exchanges:** 2 Starch, 1 Other Carbohydrate, 4 Lean Meat **Carbohydrate Choices:** 3

a new twist

It's easy to add other choices to this salad. Try adding chopped tomatoes or sliced avocado for a nice change.

apricot salsa chicken salad

Prep Time: 40 Minutes • **Start to Finish:** 55 Minutes • 4 servings

SALSA

- ⅔ cup orange juice
- ½ cup chopped dried apricots
- 2 tablespoons apricot preserves
- 1 tablespoon olive or vegetable oil
- ¾ cup chopped red bell pepper
- 2 tablespoons chopped fresh cilantro
- 2 tablespoons sliced green onions (2 medium)
- 1 teaspoon grated orange peel

SALAD

- 4 boneless skinless chicken breasts (about 1¼ lb)
- 1 tablespoon olive or vegetable oil
- ½ teaspoon garlic salt
- 6 cups bite-size pieces mixed salad greens

1 Reserve 2 tablespoons of the orange juice in small bowl; set aside. In 1-quart saucepan, heat apricots and remaining orange juice to boiling; reduce heat. Simmer uncovered 3 to 5 minutes or until most of the juice is absorbed. Cool 15 minutes.

2 Add preserves and 1 tablespoon oil to reserved 2 tablespoons orange juice. Stir in apricot mixture and remaining salsa ingredients. Refrigerate until serving time.

3 Heat gas or charcoal grill. Brush chicken with 1 tablespoon oil; sprinkle with garlic salt. Place chicken on grill over medium heat. Cover grill; cook 15 to 20 minutes, turning once, until juice of chicken is clear when center of thickest part is cut (at least 165°F). Remove chicken from grill to cutting board or plate; cut crosswise into ½-inch slices.

4 Divide salad greens among 4 plates. Top with chicken and apricot salsa.

1 Serving: Calories 340; Total Fat 12g (Saturated Fat 2g; Trans Fat 0g); Cholesterol 85mg; Sodium 230mg; Total Carbohydrate 26g (Dietary Fiber 4g); Protein 34g **Exchanges:** 1½ Other Carbohydrate, 1 Vegetable, 4 Very Lean Meat, 2 Fat **Carbohydrate Choices:** 2

swap it out

Dried peaches and peach preserves can be substituted for the dried apricots and apricot preserves. If apricot nectar is available in your area, it would make a delicious alternative to the orange juice.

cranberry chicken salad

Prep Time: 35 Minutes • **Start to Finish:** 35 Minutes • 6 servings

DRESSING

- ¾ cup mayonnaise or salad dressing
- ⅓ cup sugar
- 2 tablespoons cider vinegar
- 2 teaspoons poppy seed

CHICKEN AND SALAD

- 6 boneless skinless chicken breasts (about 1¾ lb)
  Cooking spray
- ½ teaspoon salt
- 3 cups bite-size pieces iceberg lettuce
- 3 cups bite-size pieces romaine lettuce
- ½ cup crumbled Gorgonzola cheese (2 oz)
- ½ cup sweetened dried cranberries
- 6 tablespoons slivered almonds, toasted*

1 Heat gas or charcoal grill. In small bowl, mix all dressing ingredients with whisk. Spoon ¾ cup of the dressing into separate bowl. Cover; refrigerate until serving time.

2 Spray chicken with cooking spray; sprinkle with salt. Place chicken on grill over medium heat. Cover grill; cook 15 to 20 minutes, turning once and brushing occasionally with remaining ¼ cup dressing, until juice of chicken is clear when center of thickest part is cut (at least 165°F). Discard any remaining dressing used for brushing. Remove chicken from grill to cutting board or plate; cut crosswise into ½-inch slices.

3 Divide iceberg and romaine lettuce among 6 plates. Top with chicken. Drizzle reserved ¾ cup dressing over salads. Sprinkle evenly with cheese, cranberries and almonds.

*To toast almonds, sprinkle in ungreased skillet. Cook over medium-low heat 5 to 7 minutes, stirring frequently until nuts begin to brown, then stirring constantly until nuts are light brown.

1 Serving: Calories 400; Total Fat 17g (Saturated Fat 4.5g, Trans Fat 0g); Cholesterol 115mg; Sodium 580mg; Total Carbohydrate 21g (Dietary Fiber 2g); Protein 41g **Exchanges:** 1 Other Carbohydrate, 1 Vegetable, 5½ Very Lean Meat, 3 Fat **Carbohydrate Choices**: 1½

a new twist

To make a honey-flavored dressing, omit the sugar and add ⅓ cup honey instead.

swap it out

Refrigerated coleslaw dressing can be used in place of the poppy seed dressing. Stir in 1 tablespoon poppy seed if you like.

caribbean chicken kabobs

Prep Time: 30 Minutes • **Start to Finish:** 30 Minutes • 8 servings

1¾ lb boneless skinless chicken breasts, cut into 1½-inch pieces

¼ cup vegetable oil

3 tablespoons Caribbean jerk seasoning (dry)

1 small pineapple, rind removed, cut into 1-inch cubes

1 medium red bell pepper, cut into 1-inch pieces

1 small red onion, cut into 1-inch pieces

1 Heat gas or charcoal grill. Brush chicken with 2 tablespoons of the oil. Place chicken and jerk seasoning in a resealable food-storage plastic bag. Seal bag; shake to coat chicken with seasoning.

2 On each of 8 (12-inch) metal skewers, alternately thread chicken, pineapple, bell pepper and onion, leaving ¼-inch space between each piece. Brush kabobs with remaining 2 tablespoons oil.

3 Place kabobs on grill over medium heat. Cover grill; cook 10 to 15 minutes, turning once, until chicken is no longer pink in center.

1 Serving: Calories 210; Total Fat 10g (Saturated Fat 2g; Trans Fat 0g); Cholesterol 60mg; Sodium 210mg; Total Carbohydrate 8g (Dietary Fiber 1g); Protein 22g **Exchanges:** ½ Other Carbohydrate, 3 Very Lean Meat, 1½ Fat **Carbohydrate Choices:** ½

chicken skewers with peanut sauce

Prep Time: 30 Minutes • **Start to Finish:** 1 Hour • 4 servings

CHICKEN

- 8 bamboo skewers (8 inch)
- 1 lb boneless skinless chicken breasts, cut into 1-inch pieces
- ¼ cup teriyaki marinade and sauce (from 15-oz bottle)

SAUCE

- ¼ cup creamy peanut butter
- 1 tablespoon chopped fresh cilantro
- 3 tablespoons teriyaki marinade and sauce (from 15-oz bottle)
- 1 tablespoon lime juice
- ¼ teaspoon red pepper sauce
- 4 medium green onions, chopped (¼ cup)
- 2 cloves garlic, finely chopped

RICE

- 1 cup uncooked instant brown rice
- 1¼ cups water

1 Soak bamboo skewers in water at least 30 minutes before using to prevent burning. In medium bowl, mix chicken and ¼ cup teriyaki marinade. Cover; refrigerate 30 to 60 minutes to marinate.

2 Heat gas or charcoal grill. In small bowl, stir all sauce ingredients until blended; set aside.

3 Remove chicken from marinade; discard marinade. Thread chicken on skewers. Place skewers on grill over medium heat. Cover grill; cook 10 to 15 minutes, turning once, until chicken is no longer pink in center.

4 Cook rice in water as directed on package, omitting butter and salt. Sprinkle chicken with additional chopped fresh cilantro, if desired. Serve with rice and sauce.

Broiling Directions: Set oven control to broil. Place skewered chicken on rack in broiler pan. Broil with tops 4 to 5 inches from heat 10 to 15 minutes, turning once, until chicken is no longer pink in center.

1 Serving: Calories 430; Total Fat 13g (Saturated Fat 3g; Trans Fat 0g); Cholesterol 70mg; Sodium 840mg; Total Carbohydrate 43g (Dietary Fiber 6g); Protein 34g **Exchanges:** 2 Starch, 1 Other Carbohydrate, 4 Very Lean Meat, 2 Fat **Carbohydrate Choices:** 3

mediterranean chicken-vegetable kabobs

Prep Time: 30 Minutes • **Start to Finish:** 1 Hour • 4 servings

MARINADE

- ¼ cup lemon juice
- 3 tablespoons olive or vegetable oil
- 2 teaspoons chopped fresh or 1 teaspoon dried rosemary leaves
- ½ teaspoon salt
- ¼ teaspoon pepper
- 4 cloves garlic, finely chopped

CHICKEN AND VEGETABLES

- 1 lb boneless skinless chicken breasts, cut into 1½-inch pieces
- 1 medium red bell pepper, cut into 1-inch pieces
- 1 medium zucchini or yellow summer squash, cut into 1-inch pieces
- 1 medium red onion, cut into wedges
- 1 lb fresh asparagus spears, trimmed
- ¼ cup crumbled feta cheese (1 oz)

1 In shallow glass or plastic bowl or resealable food-storage plastic bag, mix all marinade ingredients. Add chicken, stirring to coat with marinade. Cover dish or seal bag; refrigerate at least 30 minutes but no longer than 6 hours, stirring occasionally while marinating.

2 Heat gas or charcoal grill. Remove chicken from marinade; reserve marinade. On each of 4 (15-inch) metal skewers, alternately thread chicken, bell pepper, zucchini and onion, leaving ¼-inch space between each piece. Brush vegetables with reserved marinade.

3 Place kabobs on grill over medium heat. Cover grill; cook 10 to 15 minutes, turning and brushing frequently with marinade, until chicken is no longer pink in center. During last 5 minutes of cooking, add asparagus to grill, turning occasionally, until crisp-tender. Discard any remaining marinade.

4 To serve, sprinkle cheese over kabobs. Serve with asparagus.

1 Serving: Calories 250; Total Fat 9g (Saturated Fat 3g; Trans Fat 0g); Cholesterol 80mg; Sodium 250mg; Total Carbohydrate 11g (Dietary Fiber 4g); Protein 30g **Exchanges:** 2 Vegetable, 4 Very Lean Meat, 1½ Fat **Carbohydrate Choices:** 1

ranch chicken and potato packs

Prep Time: 15 Hours • **Start to Finish:** 1 Hour 5 Minutes • 4 servings

1 bag (20 oz) refrigerated cooked new potato wedges

6 boneless skinless chicken thighs (about 1¼ lb), cut in half

1¼ cups low-fat or regular ranch dressing

4 slices packaged precooked bacon (from 2.1-oz package), chopped

¼ cup chopped green onions (4 medium)

½ teaspoon coarse ground black pepper

1 Heat gas or charcoal grill. Cut 4 (18x12-inch) sheets of heavy-duty foil; spray foil with cooking spray.

2 Place about 1 cup potato wedges and 3 chicken pieces on center of each foil sheet. Drizzle each with slightly less than ⅓ cup dressing. Bring up 2 sides of foil over chicken and potatoes so edges meet. Seal edges, making tight ½-inch fold; fold again, allowing space for heat circulation and expansion.

3 Place foil packs on grill over medium heat. Cover grill; cook 45 to 50 minutes, rotating packs one half turn after 20 minutes, until juice of chicken is clear when center of thickest part is cut (at least 165°F) and potatoes are tender.

4 To serve, cut large X across top of each pack; carefully fold back foil to allow steam to escape. Sprinkle each serving with bacon, onions and pepper.

Oven Directions: Heat oven to 400°F. Place foil packs on large cookie sheet. Bake 45 to 50 minutes or until juice of chicken is clear when center of thickest part is cut (at least 165°F) and potatoes are tender.

1 Serving: Calories 570; Total Fat 29g (Saturated Fat 6g; Trans Fat 0g); Cholesterol 110mg; Sodium 930mg; Total Carbohydrate 41g (Dietary Fiber 4g); Protein 36g **Exchanges:** 2½ Starch, 4 Lean Meat, 3 Fat **Carbohydrate Choices:** 3

mediterranean chicken packs

Prep Time: 20 Minutes • **Start to Finish:** 45 Minutes • 4 servings

1 package (4 oz) crumbled tomato-basil feta cheese

2 tablespoons grated lemon peel

1 teaspoon dried oregano leaves

4 boneless skinless chicken breasts (about 1¼ lb)

4 plum (Roma) tomatoes, each cut into 3 slices

1 small red onion, finely chopped (⅓ cup)

20 pitted kalamata olives

1 Heat gas or charcoal grill. In small bowl, mix cheese, lemon peel and oregano.

2 Cut 4 (18x12-inch) sheets of heavy-duty foil; spray foil with cooking spray. Place 1 chicken breast on center of each sheet. Top each with 3 slices tomato, one-fourth of the onion, 5 olives and one-fourth of the cheese mixture. Bring up 2 sides of foil over chicken and vegetables so edges meet. Seal edges, making tight ½-inch fold; fold again, allowing space for heat circulation and expansion.

3 Place foil packs on grill over medium heat. Cover grill; cook 20 to 25 minutes, rotating packs one-half turn after 10 minutes, until juice of chicken is clear when center of thickest part is cut (at least 165°F).

4 To serve, cut large X across top of each pack; carefully fold back foil to allow steam to escape.

1 Serving: Calories 290; Total Fat 13g (Saturated Fat 6g; Trans Fat 0g); Cholesterol 115mg; Sodium 570mg; Total Carbohydrate 6g (Dietary Fiber 2g); Protein 36g **Exchanges:** ½ Vegetable, 5 Lean Meat **Carbohydrate Choices:** ½

swap it out

Plain crumbled feta cheese can be substituted for the flavored feta.

taco-spiced chicken

Prep Time: 25 Minutes   •   **Start to Finish:** 25 Minutes   •   4 servings

2 tablespoons taco seasoning mix (from 1-oz package)

1 teaspoon dried oregano leaves

4 boneless skinless chicken breasts (about 1¼ lb)

1 tablespoon olive or vegetable oil

¼ cup barbecue sauce

2 tablespoons chili sauce

½ teaspoon ground cumin

1 Heat gas or charcoal grill. In small bowl, mix taco seasoning mix and oregano. Brush chicken with oil; sprinkle with taco seasoning mixture.

2 Place chicken on grill over medium heat. Cover grill; cook 15 to 20 minutes, turning once, until juice of chicken is clear when center of thickest part is cut (at least 165°F).

3 In small microwavable bowl, mix barbecue sauce, chili sauce and cumin. Cover; microwave on High 30 to 60 seconds or until hot. Serve chicken with sauce.

Oven Directions: Heat oven to 375°F. Line shallow baking pan with foil or spray with cooking spray. Place coated chicken in pan. Bake uncovered 25 to 30 minutes until juice of chicken is clear when center of thickest part is cut (at least 165°F).

1 Serving: Calories 240; Total Fat 8g (Saturated Fat 2g; Trans Fat 0g); Cholesterol 85mg; Sodium 780mg; Total Carbohydrate 11g (Dietary Fiber 0g); Protein 31g **Exchanges:** ½ Other Carbohydrate, 4½ Very Lean Meat, 1 Fat **Carbohydrate Choices:** 1

a new twist

For zesty, make-your-own wrap sandwiches, slice the warm chicken into strips and serve with tortillas, shredded lettuce, sliced avocado and the sauce.

chicken salsa verde

Prep Time: 50 Minutes   •   **Start to Finish:** 4 Hours 50 Minutes   •   6 servings

1 tablespoon vegetable oil

3 large cloves garlic, halved

1 small onion, quartered

¾ lb tomatillos (about 7), husks removed, rinsed

1 medium to large jalapeño chile, cut in half lengthwise, seeded

¼ cup loosely packed fresh cilantro (10 to 15 sprigs)

½ teaspoon sugar

1 teaspoon salt

½ teaspoon ground cumin

6 boneless skinless chicken breasts (about 1¾ lb)

1 In 10-inch skillet, heat oil over medium-high heat. Cook garlic and onion in oil about 5 minutes, stirring frequently, until onion is tender. Remove from heat.

2 Cut around stem area of each tomatillo to remove core; cut tomatillos into quarters. In food processor, place tomatillos, garlic and onion mixture, jalapeño chile, cilantro, sugar and ½ teaspoon of the salt. Cover; process about 15 seconds or until almost smooth.

3 Pour 1 cup tomatillo salsa into small bowl; cover and refrigerate until serving time. To make marinade, add remaining ½ teaspoon salt and the cumin to remaining mixture in food processor. Cover; process 10 seconds.

4 Place chicken in shallow glass dish. Spoon and spread marinade evenly over chicken. Cover; refrigerate at least 4 hours but no longer than 8 hours, turning chicken at least once while marinating.

5 Heat gas or charcoal grill. Remove chicken from marinade; discard marinade. Carefully brush additional oil on grill rack. Place chicken on grill over medium heat. Cover grill; cook 15 to 20 minutes, turning once, until juice of chicken is clear when center of thickest part is cut (at least 165°F).

6 Serve chicken with tomatillo salsa.

1 Serving: Calories 260; Total Fat 9g (Saturated Fat 2g; Trans Fat 0g); Cholesterol 105mg; Sodium 490mg; Total Carbohydrate 6g (Dietary Fiber 1g); Protein 39g **Exchanges:** 1 Vegetable, 4 Lean Meat **Carbohydrate Choices:** ½

swap it out

In place of fresh tomatillos, you can use 3 cans (12 ounces each) whole tomatillos, drained. Decrease the salt to ½ teaspoon, using ¼ teaspoon each in the salsa and marinade.

lime- and chili-rubbed chicken breasts

Prep Time: 25 Minutes • **Start to Finish:** 25 Minutes • 4 servings

- 2 teaspoons chili powder
- 2 teaspoons packed brown sugar
- 2 teaspoons grated lime peel
- ½ teaspoon salt
- ¼ teaspoon garlic powder
- ⅛ teaspoon ground red pepper (cayenne)
- 4 boneless skinless chicken breasts (about 1¼ lb)
- 2 teaspoons olive or canola oil

1 Heat gas or charcoal grill. In small bowl, mix chili powder, brown sugar, lime peel, salt, garlic powder and red pepper. Brush both sides of chicken with oil; rub with spice mixture.

2 Place chicken on grill over medium heat. Cover grill; cook 15 to 20 minutes, turning once, until juice of chicken is clear when center of thickest part is cut (at least 165°F).

Oven Directions: Heat oven to 375°F. Line shallow baking pan with foil. Place rubbed chicken in pan. Bake uncovered 25 to 30 minutes or until juice of chicken is clear when center of thickest part is cut (at least 165°F).

1 Serving: Calories 200; Total Fat 7g (Saturated Fat 1.5g; Trans Fat 0g); Cholesterol 85mg; Sodium 390mg; Total Carbohydrate 3g (Dietary Fiber 0g); Protein 31g **Exchanges:** 4½ Very Lean Meat, 1 Fat **Carbohydrate Choices:** 0

make-ahead

Refrigerating the rubbed chicken up to 12 hours before grilling really enhances the flavor.

double-barbecue bacon-wrapped chicken

Prep Time: 35 Minutes • **Start to Finish:** 35 Minutes • 4 servings

SAUCE

- ¼ cup mayonnaise or salad dressing
- 2 teaspoons lemon juice
- 1 teaspoon cider vinegar
- 2 teaspoons chopped fresh parsley
- ¼ to ½ teaspoon red pepper sauce

CHICKEN

- 4 boneless skinless chicken breasts (about 1¼ lb)
- 8 slices packaged cooked bacon (from 2.1-oz package)
- 2 teaspoons barbecue spice
- ¼ cup barbecue sauce

1 Heat gas or charcoal grill. In small bowl, stir together all sauce ingredients. Cover; refrigerate until serving time.

2 Wrap each chicken breast with 2 slices bacon, stretching bacon to cover as much of the chicken as possible; secure ends of bacon to chicken with toothpicks. Sprinkle both sides with barbecue spice.

3 Place chicken on grill over medium heat. Cover grill; cook 5 minutes. Brush with 2 tablespoons of the barbecue sauce. Cook 10 to 15 minutes longer or until juice of chicken is clear when center of thickest part is cut (at least 165°F). Turn chicken; brush with remaining 2 tablespoons barbecue sauce.

4 Remove toothpicks. Serve chicken topped with sauce.

1 Serving: Calories 350; Total Fat 22g (Saturated Fat 5g; Trans Fat 0g); Cholesterol 95mg; Sodium 920mg; Total Carbohydrate 7g (Dietary Fiber 0g); Protein 32g **Exchanges:** ½ Starch, 3 Lean Meat, 1½ High-Fat Meat **Carbohydrate Choices:** ½

make-ahead

Make the sauce and wrap the chicken several hours ahead of time and refrigerate, then grill the chicken when needed.

cheddar-stuffed chicken breasts

Prep Time: 30 Minutes • **Start to Finish:** 30 Minutes • 4 servings

4 boneless skinless chicken breasts (about 1¼ lb)

¼ teaspoon salt

¼ teaspoon pepper

3 oz Cheddar cheese

1 tablespoon butter, melted

¼ cup chunky-style salsa

1 Heat gas or charcoal grill. Between sheets of plastic wrap or waxed paper, flatten each chicken breast to ¼–inch thickness (see page 152). Sprinkle with salt and pepper.

2 Cut cheese into 4 slices, about 3x1x¼ inch. Place 1 slice cheese in center of each chicken piece. Roll chicken around cheese, folding in sides. Brush chicken rolls with butter.

3 Place chicken rolls, seam side down, on grill over medium heat. Cover grill; cook about 15 minutes, turning after 10 minutes, until chicken is no longer pink in center. Serve chicken with salsa.

1 Serving: Calories 290; Total Fat 15g (Saturated Fat 8g; Trans Fat 0g); Cholesterol 120mg; Sodium 490mg; Total Carbohydrate 1g (Dietary Fiber 0g); Protein 37g
Exchanges: 5 Lean Meat **Carbohydrate Choices:** 0

swap it out

Add a punch to this easy chicken dish by using pepper Jack cheese instead of the Cheddar.

bourbon chicken with corn relish

Prep Time: 45 Minutes • **Start to Finish:** 45 Minutes • 6 servings

¼ cup soy sauce

¼ cup bourbon or apple cider

5 tablespoons vegetable oil

¼ cup packed brown sugar

1 tablespoon Dijon mustard

2 teaspoons red pepper sauce

1 can (15.25 oz) whole kernel sweet corn, drained

1 jar (2 oz) diced pimientos, drained

3 medium green onions, sliced (3 tablespoons)

¼ cup granulated sugar

1¼ teaspoons salt

¼ teaspoon celery seed

⅓ cup cider vinegar

6 boneless skinless chicken breasts (about 1¾ lb)

¼ teaspoon pepper

field greens, if desired

1 Heat gas or charcoal grill. In 1-quart saucepan, mix soy sauce, bourbon, 4 tablespoons of the oil, the brown sugar, mustard and pepper sauce. Heat to boiling over medium-high heat. Cook 7 to 9 minutes or until glaze is reduced to ½ cup. Remove from heat; cover to keep warm.

2 In medium bowl, mix corn, pimientos, onions and remaining 1 tablespoon oil. In another 1-quart saucepan, mix granulated sugar, ¼ teaspoon of the salt, the celery seed and vinegar. Heat to boiling; reduce heat. Simmer 2 minutes or until sugar is dissolved. Pour over corn mixture. Refrigerate until serving time.

3 Sprinkle chicken with remaining 1 teaspoon salt and the pepper. Place chicken on grill over medium heat. Cover grill; cook 15 to 20 minutes, turning once, until juice of chicken is clear when center of thickest part is cut (at least 165°F). Brush with glaze.

4 Drain corn relish. Serve each chicken breast with ¼ cup corn relish atop field greens.

1 Serving: Calories 380; Total Fat 16g (Saturated Fat 3g; Trans Fat 0g); Cholesterol 75mg; Sodium 1430mg; Total Carbohydrate 30g (Dietary Fiber 1g); Protein 29g **Exchanges:** 1½ Other Carbohydrate, 1 Vegetable, 4 Very Lean Meat, 3 Fat **Carbohydrate Choices:** 2

make-ahead

The corn relish can be made several hours ahead for the flavors to blend; refrigerate until serving time.

swap it out

During fresh corn season, substitute fresh-cut corn on the cob for the canned corn. Use a sharp knife to remove the kernels from cobs.

chicken breasts with cucumber-peach salsa

Prep Time: 30 Minutes • **Start to Finish:** 30 Minutes • 4 servings

½ cup chopped cucumber

⅓ cup peach preserves

1 tablespoon chopped fresh mint leaves or 1 teaspoon mint flakes

¼ teaspoon salt

2 tablespoons chopped red onion

1 peach or nectarine, peeled, chopped (¾ cup)

4 boneless skinless chicken breasts (about 1¼ lb)

1 Heat gas or charcoal grill. In small bowl, mix cucumber, 2 tablespoons of the preserves, the mint, salt, onion and peach; set aside.

2 Carefully brush oil on grill rack. Place chicken on grill over medium heat. Cover grill; cook 15 to 20 minutes, turning once and brushing occasionally with remaining peach preserves, until juice of chicken is clear when center of thickest part is cut (at least 165°F). Discard any remaining preserves.

3 Serve chicken with cucumber-peach salsa.

1 Serving: Calories 260; Total Fat 4.5g (Saturated Fat 1.5g; Trans Fat 0g); Cholesterol 85mg; Sodium 230mg; Total Carbohydrate 22g (Dietary Fiber 0g); Protein 32g **Exchanges:** 1½ Other Carbohydrate, 4 Very Lean Meat, ½ Fat **Carbohydrate Choices:** 1½

make-ahead

The salsa can be made up to 24 hours in advance and refrigerated. Making it ahead will also allow the flavors to blend.

raspberry-glazed chicken

Prep Time: 25 Minutes • **Start to Finish:** 25 Minutes • 6 servings

½ cup raspberry jam

1 tablespoon
Dijon mustard

6 boneless skinless chicken
breasts (about 1¾ lb)

1½ cups fresh or frozen
(thawed and drained)
raspberries

1 Heat gas or charcoal grill. In small bowl, mix jam and mustard.

2 Carefully brush oil on grill rack. Place chicken on grill over medium heat. Cover grill; cook 15 to 20 minutes, turning once and brushing frequently with jam mixture, until juice of chicken is clear when center of thickest part is cut (at least 165°F). Discard any remaining jam mixture.

3 Serve chicken topped with raspberries.

1 Serving: Calories 250; Total Fat 4.5g (Saturated Fat 1g; Trans Fat 0g); Cholesterol 80mg; Sodium 140mg; Total Carbohydrate 22g (Dietary Fiber 2g); Protein 30g **Exchanges:** ½ Fruit, 1 Other Carbohydrate, 4 Very Lean Meat, ½ Fat **Carbohydrate Choices:** 1½

chicken with lemon, rosemary and garlic

Prep Time: 25 Minutes • **Start to Finish:** 55 Minutes • 4 servings

3 tablespoons olive oil

¼ cup lemon juice

3 cloves garlic, finely chopped

2 tablespoons chopped fresh rosemary leaves

½ teaspoon salt

¼ teaspoon pepper

4 boneless skinless chicken breasts (about 1¼ lb)

1 In shallow glass or plastic dish or resealable food-storage plastic bag, mix oil, lemon juice, garlic, rosemary, salt and pepper. Add chicken, turning to coat with marinade. Cover dish or seal bag; refrigerate 30 minutes to marinate.

2 Heat gas or charcoal grill. Remove chicken from marinade; discard marinade. Place chicken on grill over medium heat. Cover grill; cook 15 to 20 minutes, turning once, until juice of chicken is clear when center of thickest part is cut (at least 165°F).

1 Serving: Calories 270; Total Fat 15g (Saturated Fat 2.5g; Trans Fat 0g); Cholesterol 90mg; Sodium 380mg; Total Carbohydrate 2g (Dietary Fiber 0g); Protein 32g
Exchanges: 4½ Very Lean Meat, 2½ Fat **Carbohydrate Choices:** 0

swap it out

Fresh thyme can be substituted for rosemary and lime juice can be used instead of the lemon juice.

sesame-ginger chicken

Prep Time: 25 Minutes • **Start to Finish:** 25 Minutes • 4 servings

2 tablespoons teriyaki sauce

1 tablespoon sesame seed, toasted*

1 teaspoon ground ginger

4 boneless skinless chicken breasts (about 1¼ lb)

1 Heat gas or charcoal grill. In small bowl, mix teriyaki sauce, sesame seed and ginger.

2 Carefully brush oil on grill rack. Place chicken on grill over medium heat. Cover grill; cook 15 to 20 minutes, turning once and brushing frequently with sauce mixture, until juice of chicken is clear when center of thickest part is cut (at least 165°F). Discard any remaining sauce mixture.

*To toast sesame seed, sprinkle in ungreased skillet. Cook over medium-low heat 5 to 7 minutes, stirring frequently until browning begins, then stirring constantly until golden brown.

1 Serving: Calories 190; Total Fat 6g (Saturated Fat 1.5g; Trans Fat 0g); Cholesterol 85mg; Sodium 420mg; Total Carbohydrate 2g (Dietary Fiber 0g); Protein 32g **Exchanges:** 4½ Very Lean Meat, 1 Fat **Carbohydrate Choices:** 0

citrus-teriyaki chicken and vegetables

Prep Time: 30 Minutes • **Start to Finish:** 1 Hour • 2 servings

¼ cup teriyaki baste and glaze (from 12-oz bottle)

¼ cup frozen (thawed) orange juice concentrate

2 teaspoons grated orange peel

½ lb uncooked chicken breast tenders (not breaded)

1 cup fresh sugar snap peas

1 cup sliced fresh mushrooms (3 oz)

1 medium zucchini, cut into ½-inch slices (2 cups)

½ medium red bell pepper, cut into 1-inch pieces (¾ cup)

1 In medium bowl, mix teriyaki glaze, orange juice concentrate and orange peel. Reserve 2 tablespoons marinade in small bowl. Add chicken to marinade in medium bowl; toss to coat. Cover; refrigerate 30 minutes to marinate.

2 Heat gas or charcoal grill. Remove chicken from marinade; discard marinade. Place chicken in grill basket (grill "wok"). Place basket on grill over medium heat. Cover grill; cook 6 to 8 minutes, shaking basket or stirring chicken occasionally, until browned.

3 Add peas, mushrooms, zucchini and bell pepper to grill basket. Cover grill; cook 6 to 8 minutes longer, shaking basket or stirring occasionally, until vegetables are crisp-tender and chicken is no longer pink in center.

4 Add 2 tablespoons reserved marinade; stir to coat vegetables and chicken. Cover grill; cook 2 to 3 minutes longer or until hot.

1 Serving: Calories 290; Total Fat 4g (Saturated Fat 1g; Trans Fat 0g); Cholesterol 70mg; Sodium 880mg; Total Carbohydrate 34g (Dietary Fiber 4g); Protein 31g **Exchanges:** 1½ Other Carbohydrate, 2 Vegetable, 4 Very Lean Meat **Carbohydrate Choices:** 2

a new twist

For a different citrus flavor, try using grated lime or lemon peel instead of the orange.

Flavorful Rubs & Marinades

RUB IN THE FLAVOR

Dry rubs are easy to make and add a big hit of instant flavor to chicken but can also be used for meat, fish and seafood. Store unused rub mixtures in airtight containers in a cool, dark location up to 6 months. Rub the mixture generously on all sides of the chicken. Cook as desired or use the Timetables for Broiling Chicken or Grilling Chicken, page 7.

Southwest Rub: Mix 2 tablespoons each regular chili powder or ground ancho chile powder, ground cumin, smoked or regular paprika, garlic powder, salt and packed brown sugar.

Caribbean Rub: Mix 1 tablespoon packed brown sugar, 1½ teaspoons ground allspice, 1 teaspoon each ground ginger and ground cinnamon, ½ teaspoon dried thyme leaves and ¼ teaspoon each salt and ground red pepper (cayenne).

Tandoori Rub: Mix 2 tablespoons each ground ginger, ground cumin, ground coriander, paprika, ground turmeric and salt with 1 tablespoon ground red pepper (cayenne).

SOAK UP THE FLAVOR

Give your chicken a good long bath in a tasty marinade for a flavor explosion! Place the desired marinade and 4 boneless skinless chicken breasts or 6 boneless skinless chicken thighs in a resealable food-storage plastic bag or shallow glass or plastic container. Seal the bag or cover the container and refrigerate at least 4 hours or up to 24 hours. Cook as desired or use the Timetables for Broiling Chicken or Grilling Chicken, page 7.

Bourbon-Maple Marinade: Mix ¼ cup each bourbon and real maple syrup, 1 tablespoon vegetable oil and ½ teaspoon salt.

Herb and Wine Marinade: Mix ½ cup each vegetable or olive oil or dry white or red wine, 2 tablespoons each fresh or 2 teaspoons each dried basil, oregano and thyme leaves, 1 tablespoon finely chopped shallots, 1 teaspoon salt and ¼ teaspoon pepper.

Coconut Curry Marinade: Mix 1 can (14 oz) coconut milk (not cream of coconut), 1 tablespoon vegetable oil, 1 tablespoon rice or cider vinegar, 1 teaspoon soy sauce, 1 tablespoon curry powder, 2 teaspoons sugar, 1 teaspoon salt and ½ teaspoon ground red pepper (cayenne).

pesto-parmesan crusted chicken

Prep Time: 45 Minutes • **Start to Finish:** 45 Minutes • 4 servings

1 tablespoon olive oil

1 teaspoon finely chopped garlic

½ cup panko crispy bread crumbs

½ cup basil pesto

3 tablespoons grated Parmesan cheese

4 bone-in chicken breasts (about 2 lb)

¼ teaspoon salt

¼ teaspoon pepper

1 Heat gas or charcoal grill. In 10-inch skillet, heat oil over medium-high heat. Cook garlic in oil about 30 seconds, stirring constantly, until fragrant. Add bread crumbs. Cook 2 to 3 minutes, stirring frequently, until toasted. Remove crumb mixture to small bowl. Stir in pesto and cheese.

2 Loosen skin on chicken to form a pocket, without detaching skin completely. Fill each pocket with pesto mixture. Sprinkle with salt and pepper.

3 Place chicken, skin side down, on grill over medium-low heat. Cover grill; cook 10 minutes, moving occasionally as needed to avoid burning the skin. Turn chicken; spoon any remaining pesto mixture over chicken. Cover grill; cook 10 to 15 minutes longer or until juice of chicken is clear when thickest part is cut to bone (at least 165°F).

1 Serving: Calories 450; Total Fat 29g (Saturated Fat 7g; Trans Fat 0g); Cholesterol 85mg; Sodium 770mg; Total Carbohydrate 12g (Dietary Fiber 1g); Protein 33g **Exchanges:** 1 Milk, 3½ Medium-Fat Meat, 1 Fat **Carbohydrate Choices:** 1

tomato-feta chicken thighs

Prep Time: 20 Minutes • **Start to Finish:** 25 Minutes • 4 servings

8   small bone-in chicken thighs (about 1½ lb)

1   tablespoon vegetable oil

½   teaspoon garlic-pepper blend

2   plum (Roma) tomatoes, each cut into 8 slices

½   cup crumbled tomato-basil feta cheese (2 oz)

1 Heat gas or charcoal grill. Brush chicken with oil; sprinkle with garlic-pepper blend.

2 Place chicken on grill over medium heat. Cover grill; cook 7 minutes. Turn chicken; top each with 2 slices tomato. Cover grill; cook about 7 minutes longer or until juice of chicken is clear when thickest part is cut to bone (at least 165°F).

3 Remove chicken from grill to serving plate; sprinkle with cheese. Cover; let stand 5 minutes to melt cheese.

1 Serving: Calories 300; Total Fat 21g (Saturated Fat 7g; Trans Fat 0g); Cholesterol 90mg; Sodium 270mg; Total Carbohydrate 2g (Dietary Fiber 0g); Protein 25g **Exchanges:** 3½ Lean Meat, 2 Fat **Carbohydrate Choices:** 0

balsamic-glazed chicken breasts

Prep Time: 35 Minutes • **Start to Finish:** 35 Minutes • 4 servings

GLAZE

- ⅓ **cup packed brown sugar**
- ⅓ **cup balsamic vinegar**
- 1 **teaspoon chopped fresh rosemary leaves**
- 1 **teaspoon finely chopped garlic**

CHICKEN

- 4 **bone-in chicken breasts (about 2 lb)**
- ½ **teaspoon salt**
- ¼ **teaspoon pepper**

1 Heat gas or charcoal grill. In small bowl, mix all glaze ingredients; set aside.

2 Sprinkle chicken with salt and pepper. Place chicken, skin side down, on grill over medium heat. Cover grill; cook 10 minutes. Turn chicken; brush with half of the glaze. Cover grill; cook 10 to 12 minutes longer, brushing frequently with glaze, until juice of chicken is clear when thickest part is cut to bone (at least 165°F). Discard any remaining glaze.

1 Serving: Calories 310; Total Fat 9g (Saturated Fat 2.5g; Trans Fat 0g); Cholesterol 95mg; Sodium 380mg; Total Carbohydrate 22g (Dietary Fiber 0g); Protein 34g **Exchanges:** 1 Other Carbohydrate, 4½ Lean Meat **Carbohydrate Choices:** 1½

a new twist

This all-purpose glaze tastes fantastic on any cut of meat. Try it on pork chops or steaks.

swap it out

Substitute any fresh herb——such as thyme, oregano, tarragon or Italian (flat-leaf) parsley—for the rosemary in this recipe.

firecracker chicken drummies

Prep Time: 35 Minutes • **Start to Finish:** 1 Hour 35 Minutes • 10 servings (about 2 wings each)

2 tablespoons chili powder

1½ teaspoons dried oregano leaves

1¼ teaspoons ground red pepper (cayenne)

1 teaspoon garlic salt

1 teaspoon ground cumin

1 teaspoon black pepper

2 lb chicken wing drummettes

Sour cream, if desired

Paprika, if desired

1 In 1-gallon resealable food-storage plastic bag, place chili powder, oregano, red pepper, garlic salt, cumin and black pepper. Seal bag; shake to blend seasonings. Add chicken; seal bag and shake until chicken is coated with seasonings. Refrigerate at least 1 hour but no longer than 24 hours to marinate.

2 Heat gas or charcoal grill. Place chicken in grill basket (grill "wok"). Place basket on grill over medium heat. Cover grill; cook 20 to 25 minutes, shaking basket to turn chicken after 10 minutes, until juice of chicken is clear when thickest part is cut to bone (at least 165°F).

3 Serve chicken with sour cream sprinkled with paprika.

1 Serving: Calories 100; Total Fat 7g (Saturated Fat 2g; Trans Fat 0g); Cholesterol 25mg; Sodium 150mg; Total Carbohydrate 1g (Dietary Fiber 0g); Protein 9g **Exchanges:** 1½ Medium-Fat Meat **Carbohydrate Choices:** 0

swap it out

Blue cheese dressing can be served instead of the sour cream and paprika.

chicken with chipotle-avocado salsa

Prep Time: 50 Minutes • **Start to Finish:** 50 Minutes • 8 servings

CHICKEN

- 1 package (1 oz) taco seasoning mix
- 2 tablespoons olive oil
- 2 tablespoons lime juice
- 1 tablespoon honey
- 2 quartered whole chickens (3 to 3½ lb each), skin and fat removed if desired

SALSA

- 1 medium tomato, chopped
- 1 medium avocado, pitted, peeled and chopped
- 2 tablespoons chopped fresh cilantro
- 2 tablespoons finely chopped red onion
- ½ teaspoon garlic salt
- 1 to 2 teaspoons chopped chipotle chiles in adobo sauce (from 7-oz can)

1 Heat gas or charcoal grill. In medium bowl, stir taco seasoning mix, oil, lime juice and honey until well blended. Brush mixture evenly over all sides of chicken.

2 Place chicken on grill over medium heat. Cover grill; cook 30 to 40 minutes, turning frequently, until juice of chicken is clear when thickest pieces are cut to bone (at least 165°F).

3 In medium bowl, mix all salsa ingredients. Serve chicken with salsa.

Broiling Directions: Set oven control to broil. Brush chicken with taco seasoning mixture. Place on broiler pan. Broil with tops 4 to 6 inches from heat 30 to 40 minutes, turning frequently, until juice of chicken is clear when thickest pieces are cut to bone (at least 165°F).

1 Serving: Calories 340; Total Fat 16g (Saturated Fat 3.5g; Trans Fat 0g); Cholesterol 120mg; Sodium 430mg; Total Carbohydrate 7g (Dietary Fiber 2g); Protein 40g **Exchanges:** ½ Other Carbohydrate, 5½ Lean Meat, **Carbohydrate Choices:** ½

swap it out

You can substitute bone-in chicken breasts for the chicken quarters if you like.

beer-brined chicken

Prep Time: 15 Minutes ▪ **Start to Finish:** 10 Hours ▪ 8 servings

BRINE AND CHICKEN

- 2 cups water
- ¼ cup kosher (coarse) salt
- ¼ cup packed brown sugar
- 4 cans or bottles (12 oz each) regular or nonalcoholic beer, chilled
- 2 cut-up whole chickens (3 to 3½ lb each)

BARBECUE RUB

- 1 tablespoon paprika
- 1 teaspoon table salt
- ½ teaspoon onion powder
- ½ teaspoon garlic powder
- ½ teaspoon pepper
- ¼ cup vegetable oil

1 In 6- to 8-quart noncorrosive (stainless steel, enamel-coated or plastic) container or stockpot, mix water, kosher salt and brown sugar, stirring until salt and sugar are dissolved. Stir in beer. Add chicken. Cover; refrigerate at least 8 hours but no longer than 24 hours.

2 Line 15x10x1-inch pan with foil. Remove chicken from brine; rinse thoroughly under cool running water and pat dry with paper towels. Discard brine. Place chicken in pan. Refrigerate uncovered 1 hour to dry chicken skin. Meanwhile, in small bowl, mix all rub ingredients except oil; set aside.

3 Brush oil over chicken; sprinkle rub mixture over chicken. Heat gas or charcoal grill for indirect cooking. For two-burner gas grill, heat one burner to medium; place chicken on unheated side. For one-burner gas grill, place chicken on grill over low heat. For charcoal grill, move medium coals to edge of firebox; place chicken over drip pan.

4 Cover grill; cook 15 minutes. Turn chicken. Cover grill; cook 20 to 30 minutes longer, turning occasionally, until juice of chicken is clear when thickest pieces are cut to bone (at least 165°F).

Oven Directions: Make chicken as directed through step 2. Heat oven to 425°F. Brush oil over chicken; sprinkle rub mixture over chicken. Bake uncovered 25 to 35 minutes or until juice of chicken is clear when thickest pieces are cut to bone (at least 165°F).

1 Serving: Calories 380; Total Fat 24g (Saturated Fat 6g; Trans Fat 0.5g); Cholesterol 130mg; Sodium 900mg; Total Carbohydrate 0g (Dietary Fiber 0g); Protein 40g **Exchanges:** 5½ Lean Meat, 1½ Fat **Carbohydrate Choices:** 0

beer can chicken

Prep Time: 10 Minutes • **Start to Finish:** 1 Hour 55 Minutes • 6 servings

RUB

- 1 tablespoon paprika
- 2 teaspoons salt
- ½ teaspoon garlic powder
- ½ teaspoon onion powder
- ½ teaspoon pepper

CHICKEN

- 1 whole chicken (4 to 4½ lb)
- 1 can (12 oz) regular or nonalcoholic beer

1 In small bowl, mix all rub ingredients. Fold wings of chicken across back with tips touching. Sprinkle rub inside cavity and all over outside of chicken; rub with fingers.

2 Pour out ½ cup of beer from can. Holding chicken upright with larger opening of body cavity downward; insert beer can into larger cavity. Insert ovenproof meat, grilling or digital thermometer so tip is in thickest part of inside thigh and does not touch bone.

3 Heat gas or charcoal grill for indirect cooking. For two-burner gas grill, heat one burner to medium; place chicken with beer can upright on unheated side. For one-burner gas grill, place chicken on grill over low heat. For charcoal grill, move medium coals to edge of firebox; place chicken on grill rack over drip pan.

4 Cover grill; cook 1 hour 15 minutes to 1 hour 30 minutes or until thermometer reads at least 165°F and legs move easily when lifted or twisted. Using tongs, carefully lift chicken to 13x9-inch pan, holding large metal spatula under beer can for support. Let stand 15 minutes before carving. Remove beer can; discard.

1 Serving: Calories 300; Total Fat 18g (Saturated Fat 5g; Trans Fat 0.5g); Cholesterol 115mg; Sodium 700mg; Total Carbohydrate 0g (Dietary Fiber 0g); Protein 36g
Exchanges: 5 Lean Meat, 1 Fat **Carbohydrate Choices:** 0

CHAPTER 2

In the Oven

herb roast chicken and vegetables

Prep Time: 20 Minutes • **Start to Finish:** 2 Hours 5 Minutes • 6 servings

¼ cup olive or vegetable oil

2 tablespoons chopped fresh or 1 teaspoon dried thyme leaves

2 tablespoons chopped fresh or 1 teaspoon dried marjoram leaves

½ teaspoon salt

¼ teaspoon coarse ground black pepper

1 lemon

1 whole chicken (4 to 5 lb)

6 small red potatoes, cut in half

1 cup ready-to-eat baby-cut carrots

8 oz fresh green beans, trimmed

1 Heat oven to 375°F. In small bowl, mix oil, thyme, marjoram, salt and pepper. Grate 1 teaspoon peel from lemon; stir into oil mixture. Cut lemon into quarters; place in cavity of chicken.

2 Fold wings across back of chicken so tips are touching. Skewer or tie legs together. On rack in shallow roasting pan or 13x9-inch pan fitted with rack, place chicken, breast side up. Brush some of the oil mixture on chicken. Insert ovenproof meat thermometer so tip is in thickest part of thigh and does not touch bone.

3 Roast uncovered 45 minutes. Arrange potatoes, carrots and green beans around chicken; brush remaining oil mixture on chicken and vegetables. Roast uncovered 30 to 45 minutes longer or until thermometer reads at least 165°F, legs move easily when lifted or twisted and vegetables are tender. Cover loosely with foil; let stand 15 minutes before carving.

4 Remove lemon and discard. Place chicken on platter; arrange vegetables around chicken. Serve with pan drippings.

Carving a Whole Chicken

Remove ties or skewers.

Hold drumstick; cut through joint and between thigh and body.

Remove wing from body by cutting through wing joint.

Just to right of breast, cut through meat to remove; slice.

moroccan spatchcocked chicken

Prep Time: 20 Minutes • **Start to Finish:** 1 Hour 30 Minutes • 4 servings

1 whole chicken (3½ to 4½ lb)

1½ teaspoons ground cumin

1¼ teaspoons salt

¼ teaspoon ground cinnamon

¼ cup honey

2 tablespoons olive oil

2 tablespoons pomegranate molasses

¼ cup pomegranate seeds

Chopped fresh cilantro, if desired

1 Heat oven to 400°F. Line 15x10x1-inch pan with foil.

2 Pat chicken dry with paper towels. Place chicken, breast side down, on cutting board. Using heavy-duty kitchen scissors or poultry shears, cut closely along one side of backbone from thigh end to neck. Repeat on other side. Remove backbone; save for making Chicken and Broth (page 192) or Roasted Chicken and Broth (page 194) or discard. Turn chicken over; flatten breast area by pressing firmly with heel of hand. Place chicken, breast side up, in pan. Tuck wings under breast.

3 In small bowl, mix cumin, salt and cinnamon; sprinkle evenly over chicken. Cover with foil; bake 50 minutes. In another small bowl, mix honey, oil and molasses until well blended. Brush mixture on chicken.

4 Bake uncovered 10 to 20 minutes longer, brushing once or twice with pan juices, or until thermometer inserted in thickest part of breast reads at least 165°F. Sprinkle chicken with pomegranate seeds and cilantro. Serve with pan juices, if desired.

1 Serving: Calories 430; Total Fat 17g (Saturated Fat 4g; Trans Fat 0g); Cholesterol 125mg; Sodium 860mg; Total Carbohydrate 27g (Dietary Fiber 0g); Protein 40g **Exchanges:** 2 Other Carbohydrate, 5½ Lean Meat **Carbohydrate Choices:** 2

swap it out

Try our easy homemade version of pomegranate molasses. In 2-quart stainless steel saucepan, stir 4 cups plain pomegranate juice, ⅓ cup sugar and 2 teaspoons lemon juice. Cook over medium heat 2 to 3 minutes, stirring occasionally, until sugar is dissolved. Reduce heat to medium-low. Cook uncovered 1½ hours, stirring occasionally, until reduced to 1 cup and consistency is like thick syrup. Remove from heat. Let stand at room temperature 30 minutes. Transfer to jar, but do not cover; cool completely. Cover; refrigerate up to 3 months.

Spatchcocked (Butterflied) Chicken

No doubt about it, spatchcock is a whimsical-sounding name, right up there with snickerdoodle cookies and whoopie pies. Spatchcocking is thought to date back to 18th-century Ireland and is making a big comeback. The term describes the method of removing the backbone of a whole chicken or other fowl, turning it over, and pressing it flat so it looks like an opened book. You are butterflying the chicken. This technique lets you cook a whole chicken in less time, and it's a great conversation starter!

Check out the step-by-step photos below for how to spatchcock a chicken. The test kitchen testers were amazed at how easy and fast this technique was to do, and no special equipment is needed, just a kitchen scissors or poultry shears—both cut through the chicken with ease. There are two delicious recipes for you to try, Moroccan Spatchcocked Chicken (page 64) and Herb-Garlic Butter Spatchcocked Chicken (page 68).

Spatchcocking a Chicken

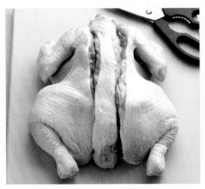

Place chicken, breast side down, on cutting board. Using heavy-duty kitchen scissors or poultry shears, cut closely along one side of backbone from thigh end to neck.

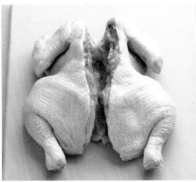

Repeat on other side, and remove backbone.

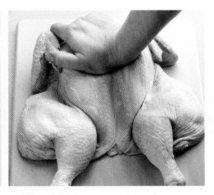

Turn chicken over. Flatten breast area by pressing firmly with heel of hand.

Making Herb-Garlic Butter Spatchcocked Chicken

Using fingers, rub half of butter mixture under skin to cover entire breast area. Gently replace skin.

Rub remaining butter mixture on outside of chicken.

herb-garlic butter spatchcocked chicken

Prep Time: 20 Minutes   •   **Start to Finish:** 1 Hour 25 Minutes   •   4 servings

1   whole chicken (3½ to 4½ lb)

⅓   cup butter, softened

3   tablespoons chopped fresh or 1 tablespoon dried herb leaves (basil, chives, oregano, tarragon or thyme, or a combination)

5   teaspoons lemon juice

½   teaspoon salt

2   cloves garlic, finely chopped

1 Heat oven to 375°F. Line 15x10x1-inch pan with foil.

2 Pat chicken dry with paper towels. Place chicken, breast side down, on cutting board. Using heavy-duty kitchen scissors or poultry shears, cut closely along one side of backbone from thigh end to neck. Repeat on other side. Remove backbone; save for making Chicken and Broth (page 192) or Roasted Chicken and Broth (page 194) or discard. Turn chicken over; flatten breast area by pressing firmly with heel of hand. Place chicken, breast side up, in pan. Tuck wings under breast.

3 In small bowl, beat remaining ingredients with electric mixer on medium speed until light and fluffy. Starting at leg end of chicken, gently separate skin (do not peel back) from chicken breast using fingers, being careful not to tear or puncture skin. Rub half of butter mixture under skin to cover entire breast area; gently replace skin. Rub remaining butter mixture on outside of chicken.

4 Roast uncovered 30 minutes. Brush chicken with pan juices. Roast 30 to 35 minutes longer or until thermometer inserted in thickest part of breast reads at least 165°F. Serve chicken with pan juices, if desired.

1 Serving: Calories 400; Total Fat 26g (Saturated Fat 13g; Trans Fat 1g); Cholesterol 165mg; Sodium 550mg; Total Carbohydrate 0g (Dietary Fiber 0g); Protein 40g **Exchanges:** 5½ Lean Meat, 2 Fat **Carbohydrate Choices:** 0

make-ahead

The herb-garlic butter can be made 1 day ahead of time and refrigerated. Soften the butter at room temperature before preparing the chicken.

oven-fried ranch chicken

Prep Time: 10 Minutes • **Start to Finish:** 1 Hour 50 Minutes • **4 servings**

CHICKEN

- 2 cups buttermilk
- 2 packages (1 oz each) ranch salad dressing mix
- 1 cut-up whole chicken (3 to 3½ lb)
  Cooking spray

BREADING

- 1 pouch (6.5 oz) cornbread & muffin mix
- 1 teaspoon paprika
- 1 teaspoon pepper
- ½ teaspoon seasoned salt
- ⅛ teaspoon ground red pepper (cayenne)
  Fresh parsley sprigs, if desired

1 In large resealable food-storage plastic bag, mix buttermilk, dressing mix and chicken. Seal bag; turn bag several times to coat chicken. Refrigerate at least 1 hour.

2 Heat oven to 425°F. Spray 15x10x1-inch pan with cooking spray. In shallow dish, mix all breading ingredients. Remove chicken pieces one at a time from buttermilk mixture. Dip chicken in breading, turning to coat completely; shake off excess. Place chicken, bone side down, in pan. Lightly spray top of chicken with cooking spray.

3 Bake 35 to 40 minutes until juice of chicken is clear when thickest pieces are cut to bone (at least 165°F). Garnish with parsley sprigs.

1 Serving: Calories 610; Total Fat 23g (Saturated Fat 6g; Trans Fat 0.5g); Cholesterol 135mg; Sodium 1770mg; Total Carbohydrate 51g (Dietary Fiber 0g); Protein 49g
Exchanges: 2 Starch, 1 Other Carbohydrate, ½ Low-Fat Milk, 5 Lean Meat, 1 Fat
Carbohydrate Choices: 3½

a new twist

For an Italian-flavored chicken, use a .7-ounce package of regular or .6-ounce package of zesty Italian salad dressing mix instead of the ranch salad dressing mix.

swap it out

If you don't have buttermilk on hand, pour 2 tablespoons vinegar or lemon juice into a 2-cup measuring cup and add enough milk to measure 2 cups. Stir, then let stand for 5 minutes.

parmesan oven-fried chicken

Prep Time: 10 Minutes • **Start to Finish:** 1 Hour • 6 servings

1	tablespoon butter
½	cup grated Parmesan cheese
⅓	cup Original Bisquick™ mix
1½	teaspoons paprika
1	teaspoon Italian seasoning, if desired
1	teaspoon salt
¼	teaspoon pepper
1	cut-up whole chicken (3 to 3½ lb)

1 Heat oven to 425°F. In 13x9-inch pan, melt butter in oven.

2 In shallow dish, stir together cheese, Bisquick mix, paprika, Italian seasoning, salt and pepper. Coat chicken with mixture. Place chicken, skin side down, over butter in hot pan.

3 Bake uncovered 35 minutes. Turn chicken; bake about 15 minutes longer or until juice of chicken is clear when thickest pieces are cut to bone (at least 165°F).

1 Serving: Calories 280; Total Fat 13g (Saturated Fat 5g; Trans Fat 1g); Cholesterol 80mg; Sodium 870mg; Total Carbohydrate 14g (Dietary Fiber 0g); Protein 28g **Exchanges:** 1 Other Carbohydrate, 4 Lean Meat **Carbohydrate Choices:** 1

make-ahead

Leftover chicken keeps for up to 3 days in the refrigerator, so go ahead and double the recipe. When you have extra chicken on hand, you're only moments away from an impromptu picnic since this chicken is delicious cold, too.

green bean and chicken casserole

Prep Time: 10 Minutes • **Start to Finish:** 55 Minutes • 4 servings

1 can (10¾ oz) condensed cream of chicken soup

¼ cup milk

1 cup herb-seasoned stuffing crumbs

¼ cup butter, melted

1¼ lb boneless skinless chicken breasts, cut crosswise into 1-inch strips

2 cups frozen cut green beans (from 12-oz bag), thawed

1 Heat oven to 350°F. Lightly spray 11x7-inch (2-quart) glass baking dish with cooking spray.

2 In small bowl, mix soup and milk until well blended. In another small bowl, mix stuffing crumbs and melted butter.

3 In baking dish, layer chicken, green beans, soup mixture and stuffing mixture.

4 Bake uncovered about 45 minutes or until hot and bubbly and chicken is no longer pink in center.

1 Serving: Calories 450; Total Fat 23g (Saturated Fat 11g; Trans Fat 1g); Cholesterol 125mg; Sodium 1000mg; Total Carbohydrate 25g (Dietary Fiber 2g); Protein 37g **Exchanges:** 1½ Starch, 1 Vegetable, 4 Very Lean Meat, 4 Fat **Carbohydrate Choices:** 1½

chicken tortilla casserole

Prep Time: 20 Minutes • **Start to Finish:** 1 Hour 15 Minutes • 8 servings

1 can (10¾ oz) 98% fat-free condensed cream of chicken soup with 45% less sodium

1 can (4.5 oz) chopped green chiles

1 container (8 oz) fat-free sour cream

½ cup fat-free (skim) milk

2½ cups shredded cooked chicken breast

8 soft corn tortillas (6 or 7 inch), torn into bite-size pieces

1 medium green bell pepper, chopped (1 cup)

1 large tomato, chopped (1 cup)

1½ cups shredded sharp Cheddar cheese or Mexican cheese blend (6 oz)

1 Heat oven to 350°F. Spray 13x9-inch (3-quart) glass baking dish with cooking spray.

2 In large bowl, mix soup, chiles, sour cream and milk until blended. Stir in chicken, tortillas and bell pepper. Stir in tomato and 1 cup of the cheese. Spread mixture in baking dish.

3 Cover with foil; bake 40 minutes. Uncover; sprinkle with remaining ½ cup cheese. Bake 5 to 10 minutes longer or until cheese is melted and mixture is bubbly. Let stand 5 minutes before serving.

1 Serving: Calories 270; Total Fat 11g (Saturated Fat 5g; Trans Fat 0g); Cholesterol 60mg; Sodium 610mg; Total Carbohydrate 22g (Dietary Fiber 2g); Protein 22g **Exchanges:** 1½ Starch, 2½ Very Lean Meat, 1½ Fat **Carbohydrate Choices:** 1½

baked chicken panzanella

Prep Time: 10 Minutes • **Start to Finish:** 40 Minutes • 6 servings (1½ cups each)

2 cups chopped cooked chicken

1 can (14.5 oz) diced tomatoes with garlic, onion and oregano, drained

4 medium green onions, sliced (¼ cup)

1 package (5 oz) Italian-seasoned croutons

¼ cup Italian dressing

¾ cup shredded Parmesan cheese (3 oz)

¼ cup sliced fresh basil leaves

1 Heat oven to 350°F. In ungreased 11x7-inch (2-quart) glass baking dish, layer chicken, tomatoes, green onions and croutons. Drizzle with Italian dressing.

2 Cover with foil; bake 20 minutes. Uncover; top with cheese. Bake about 10 minutes longer or until hot and cheese is melted. Sprinkle with basil.

1 Serving: Calories 290; Total Fat 14g (Saturated Fat 4.5g; Trans Fat 1.5g); Cholesterol 50mg; Sodium 830mg; Total Carbohydrate 20g (Dietary Fiber 2g); Protein 21g **Exchanges:** 1 Starch, ½ Other Carbohydrate, 2½ Medium-Fat Meat **Carbohydrate Choices:** 1

swap it out

Any cooked chicken will work in this recipe. Use deli rotisserie chicken or refrigerated cubed cooked chicken. Or use leftover grilled chicken, which would add a slightly smoky flavor to the casserole.

chicken and veggie risotto bake

Prep Time: 30 Minutes • **Start to Finish:** 1 Hour 30 Minutes • 8 servings

¼ cup butter

2 medium onions, chopped (1 cup)

1 tablespoon finely chopped garlic

1½ cups uncooked short-grain Arborio rice

1 medium sweet potato, peeled, cut into ½-inch pieces (2 cups)

2 medium parsnips, peeled, cut into ½-inch pieces (1 cup)

3 medium carrots, cut into ½-inch slices (1 cup)

4½ cups chicken broth

2 teaspoons chopped fresh thyme leaves

1½ teaspoons chopped fresh rosemary leaves

3 cups shredded cooked chicken

¾ cup shredded Parmesan cheese (3 oz)

¼ cup whipping cream

½ teaspoon salt

¼ teaspoon pepper

1 Heat oven to 400°F. Spray 13x9-inch pan with cooking spray.

2 In 12-inch skillet, melt 2 tablespoons butter over medium heat. Cook onion in butter 5 minutes, stirring frequently, until tender. Stir in garlic and rice; cook 1 minute. Spoon mixture into baking dish.

3 In same skillet, melt remaining 2 tablespoons butter over medium heat. Cook sweet potatoes, parsnips and carrots in butter 6 minutes, stirring occasionally. Spoon vegetables over rice mixture. Add broth, thyme and rosemary to skillet. Stir in chicken, cheese, whipping cream, salt and pepper. Add to baking dish; stir until well combined.

4 Cover; bake 1 hour or until rice and vegetables are tender and most of liquid is absorbed.

1 Serving: Calories 400; Total Fat 14g (Saturated Fat 8g; Trans Fat 0g); Cholesterol 0mg; Sodium 850mg; Total Carbohydrate 37g (Dietary Fiber 3g); Protein 30g **Exchanges:** 2 Starch, 1 Vegetable, 2 Very Lean Meat, 1 High-Fat Meat **Carbohydrate Choices:** 2½

chicken tetrazzini

Prep Time: 25 Minutes • **Start to Finish:** 55 Minutes • 6 servings

1 package (7 oz) uncooked spaghetti, broken into thirds

2 cups frozen sweet peas (from 12-oz bag)

¼ cup butter

¼ cup all-purpose flour

½ teaspoon salt

¼ teaspoon pepper

1 cup chicken broth

1 cup whipping cream

2 tablespoons dry sherry or water

2 cups cubed deli rotisserie chicken (from 2- to 3-lb chicken)

1 jar (4.5 oz) sliced mushrooms, drained

½ cup grated Parmesan cheese

1 Heat oven to 350°F. Cook and drain spaghetti as directed on package, using minimum cook time and adding frozen peas during last 3 minutes of cooking.

2 Meanwhile, in 3-quart saucepan, melt butter over low heat. Stir in flour, salt and pepper. Cook and stir until mixture is smooth and bubbly; remove from heat.

3 Stir in broth and whipping cream. Heat to boiling, stirring constantly. Boil and stir 1 minute. Stir in sherry, spaghetti and peas, chicken and mushrooms. Spoon mixture into ungreased 2-quart casserole. Sprinkle with cheese.

4 Bake uncovered about 30 minutes or until bubbly in center.

1 Serving: Calories 500; Total Fat 27g (Saturated Fat 15g; Trans Fat 1g); Cholesterol 110mg; Sodium 1030mg; Total Carbohydrate 40g (Dietary Fiber 4g); Protein 26g **Exchanges:** 2 Starch, ½ Other Carbohydrate, 1 Vegetable, 2½ Lean Meat, 3½ Fat **Carbohydrate Choices:** 2½

make-ahead

Make this casserole the night before; cover and refrigerate until ready to bake. It may need to bake an additional 10 minutes to become bubbly in the center.

creamy chicken lasagna

Prep Time: 40 Minutes • **Start to Finish:** 1 Hour 50 Minutes • 8 servings

12 uncooked lasagna noodles

1 tablespoon butter

¾ cup chopped green bell pepper

¾ cup chopped onion

⅓ cup milk

2 cans (10¾ oz each) condensed cream of chicken soup

½ teaspoon dried basil leaves

¼ teaspoon pepper

1 container (12 oz) small-curd cottage cheese

3 cups diced skinned deli rotisserie chicken (from 2- to 3-lb chicken)

2 cups shredded mozzarella cheese (8 oz)

1 cup shredded Cheddar cheese (4 oz)

½ cup grated Parmesan cheese

1 Heat oven to 350°F. Spray 13x9-inch (3-quart) glass baking dish with cooking spray. Cook and drain noodles as directed on package.

2 Meanwhile, in 3-quart saucepan, melt butter over medium-high heat. Add bell pepper and onion; cook about 5 minutes, stirring occasionally, until crisp-tender. Remove from heat. Stir in milk, soup, basil and pepper.

3 Place 4 noodles in baking dish. Top with about 1 cup of the soup mixture, half of the cottage cheese, 1½ cups of the chicken, ⅔ cup of the mozzarella cheese and ⅓ cup of the Cheddar cheese. Repeat layers once, starting with noodles. Place remaining 4 noodles over top. Top with remaining soup mixture, mozzarella cheese and Cheddar cheese. Sprinkle Parmesan cheese over top.

4 Bake uncovered 50 to 55 minutes or until center is hot and top is golden brown. Let stand 15 minutes before cutting.

1 Serving: Calories 520; Total Fat 24g (Saturated Fat 12g; Trans Fat 0.5g); Cholesterol 95mg; Sodium 1460mg; Total Carbohydrate 36g (Dietary Fiber 2g); Protein 41g **Exchanges:** 2½ Starch, 4½ Lean Meat, 2 Fat **Carbohydrate Choices:** 2½

swap it out

Ricotta cheese can be substituted for the cottage cheese.

chicken- and spinach-stuffed shells

Prep Time: 30 Minutes • **Start to Finish:** 1 Hour 10 Minutes • 6 servings (3 shells each)

18 uncooked jumbo pasta shells (from 16-oz box)

1 container (15 oz) whole-milk ricotta cheese

1 egg, slightly beaten

¼ cup grated Parmesan cheese

2 cups frozen cut leaf spinach (from 1-lb bag), thawed, squeezed to drain

1 cup chopped cooked chicken

1 jar (26 oz) tomato pasta sauce

2 cups shredded Italian cheese blend (8 oz)

1 Heat oven to 350°F. Cook and drain pasta as directed on package. Rinse with cold water to cool; drain.

2 Meanwhile, in medium bowl, mix ricotta cheese, egg, Parmesan cheese, spinach and chicken.

3 Spread 1 cup of the pasta sauce in bottom of ungreased 13x9-inch (3-quart) glass baking dish. Spoon about 2 tablespoons ricotta mixture into each pasta shell. Arrange shells, filled side up, on sauce in baking dish. Spoon remaining sauce over stuffed shells.

4 Cover with foil; bake 30 minutes. Uncover; sprinkle with Italian cheese. Bake 5 to 10 minutes longer or until cheese is melted.

1 Serving: Calories 570; Total Fat 28g (Saturated Fat 15g; Trans Fat 0.5g); Cholesterol 120mg; Sodium 1330mg; Total Carbohydrate 48g (Dietary Fiber 4g); Protein 33g **Exchanges:** 3 Starch, 1 Vegetable, 3 Medium-Fat Meat, 2 Fat **Carbohydrate Choices:** 3

make-ahead

Make as directed through step 3. Cover tightly and refrigerate up to 24 hours. Add 5 to 10 minutes to the first bake time before topping with cheese.

sage chicken and potatoes

Prep Time: 15 Minutes • **Start to Finish:** 1 Hour 15 Minutes • 4 servings

4 boneless skinless chicken breasts (about 1¼ lb)

3 medium unpeeled baking potatoes, cut into ¾-inch pieces (3 cups)

1½ cups ready-to-eat baby-cut carrots

1 jar (12 oz) home-style chicken gravy

2 tablespoons Worcestershire sauce

1 teaspoon dried sage leaves

½ teaspoon garlic-pepper blend

1 Heat oven to 400°F. Spray 13x9-inch (3-quart) glass baking dish with cooking spray. Arrange chicken, potatoes and carrots in baking dish.

2 In small bowl, mix gravy, Worcestershire sauce, sage and garlic-pepper blend. Pour mixture over chicken and vegetables. Spray sheet of foil with cooking spray; cover baking dish with foil, sprayed side down.

3 Bake 50 to 60 minutes or until vegetables are tender and juice of chicken is clear when center of thickest part is cut (at least 165°F).

1 Serving: Calories 320; Total Fat 9g (Saturated Fat 2.5g; Trans Fat 0g); Cholesterol 75mg; Sodium 680mg; Total Carbohydrate 30g (Dietary Fiber 4g); Protein 31g **Exchanges:** 2 Starch, 3½ Very Lean Meat, 1 Fat **Carbohydrate Choices:** 2

swap it out

You can use bone-in chicken breasts, but they will take a little longer to bake. Check to see if they're done by cutting the thickest part of the chicken to the bone; the juice should be clear.

oven chicken cordon bleu

Prep Time: 20 Minutes • **Start to Finish:** 50 Minutes • 4 servings

4 boneless skinless chicken breasts (about 1¼ lb)

2 teaspoons Dijon mustard

4 teaspoons chopped fresh chives

4 thin slices (about ¾ oz each) lean cooked ham

4 thin slices (about ¾ oz each) reduced-fat Swiss cheese

1 egg white

1 tablespoon water

⅓ cup finely crushed corn flakes or bran flakes cereal

¼ teaspoon paprika

1 Heat oven to 375°F. Spray 8-inch square (2 quart) glass baking dish with cooking spray. Between sheets of plastic wrap or waxed paper, flatten each chicken breast to ¼-inch thickness (see page 152).

2 Spread each chicken breast with ½ teaspoon mustard; sprinkle with 1 teaspoon chives. Cut ham and cheese slices to fit chicken. Top each chicken breast with ham and cheese slice. Roll up, tucking ends inside.

3 In shallow dish, slightly beat egg white and water. Place cereal crumbs in another shallow dish. Coat chicken rolls with egg white mixture; roll in crumbs. Place in baking dish. Sprinkle with paprika.

4 Bake uncovered 25 to 30 minutes or until chicken is no longer pink in center.

1 Serving: Calories 150; Total Fat 4g (Saturated Fat 1.5g; Trans Fat 0g); Cholesterol 60mg; Sodium 440mg; Total Carbohydrate 2g (Dietary Fiber 0g); Protein 25g **Exchanges:** 3 Lean Meat **Carbohydrate Choices:** 0

parmesan-dijon chicken

Prep Time: 10 Minutes • **Start to Finish:** 40 Minutes • 6 servings

¼ cup butter, melted

2 tablespoons Dijon mustard

¾ cup seasoned dry bread crumbs

¼ cup grated Parmesan cheese

6 boneless skinless chicken breasts (about 1¾ lb)

1 Heat oven to 375°F. In shallow dish, mix melted butter and mustard. In large resealable food-storage plastic bag, mix bread crumbs and cheese.

2 Dip chicken, one piece at a time, into butter mixture, coating all sides. Place in bag of bread crumbs; seal bag and shake to coat with crumb mixture. Place chicken in ungreased 13x9-inch pan.

3 Bake uncovered 20 to 30 minutes, turning once, until juice of chicken is clear when center of thickest part is cut (at least 165°F).

1 Serving: Calories 340; Total Fat 15g (Saturated Fat 7g; Trans Fat 0g); Cholesterol 125mg; Sodium 620mg; Total Carbohydrate 10g (Dietary Fiber 0g); Protein 41g **Exchanges:** ½ Starch, ½ Very Lean Meat, 5 Lean Meat **Carbohydrate Choices:** ½

a new twist

Go ahead and add a pinch of this or a dash of that. Try adding dried basil, thyme, sage or rosemary leaves, dried dill weed or seasoned salt to taste to the bread crumb mixture.

cheese-stuffed buffalo chicken rolls

Prep Time: 25 Minutes • **Start to Finish:** 1 Hour • **4 servings**

4   boneless skinless chicken breasts (about 1¼ lb)

¼   teaspoon salt

¼   cup finely crumbled blue cheese (1 oz)

¼   cup finely shredded Cheddar cheese (1 oz)

2   tablespoons butter, melted

2   tablespoons Buffalo wing sauce

⅓   cup unseasoned dry bread crumbs

Blue cheese dressing, if desired

Celery sticks, if desired

1 Heat oven to 375°F. Spray 15x10x1-inch pan with cooking spray. Between sheets of plastic wrap or waxed paper, flatten each chicken breast to ¼-inch thickness (see page 152). Sprinkle with salt.

2 Place 1 tablespoon blue cheese and 1 tablespoon Cheddar cheese in center of each chicken breast to within ½ inch of short sides. Fold short sides about 1 inch toward center. Starting at long side, roll chicken over cheese, tucking in sides as needed. Secure ends with toothpicks.

3 In shallow dish, mix melted butter and Buffalo wing sauce until well blended. Place bread crumbs in another shallow dish. Coat chicken rolls with butter mixture; roll in crumbs. Place seam side down in pan.

4 Bake 25 to 35 minutes or until chicken is no longer pink in center. Remove toothpicks. Serve chicken with blue cheese dressing and celery.

1 Serving: Calories 350; Total Fat 17g (Saturated Fat 9g; Trans Fat 0g); Cholesterol 130mg; Sodium 620mg; Total Carbohydrate 7g (Dietary Fiber 0g); Protein 42g **Exchanges:** ½ Other Carbohydrate, 5½ Very Lean Meat, ½ High-Fat Meat, 2 Fat **Carbohydrate Choices:** ½

make-ahead

Make chicken rolls as directed through step 2. Cover and refrigerate up to 24 hours before baking. Continue as directed in steps 3 and 4.

swap it out

For a bolder, hotter flavor, use pepper Jack instead of Cheddar cheese.

Rolling Up Chicken Rolls

Fold short sides about 1 inch toward center.

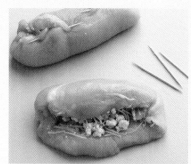

Roll chicken over cheese, tucking in sides as needed. Secure ends with toothpicks.

stuffed chicken parmesan

Prep Time: 25 Minutes • **Start to Finish:** 1 Hour • 6 servings

6 boneless skinless chicken breasts (about 1¾ lb)

1 box (10 oz) frozen cut spinach, thawed, well drained

2 oz ⅓-less-fat cream cheese (Neufchâtel), softened

¼ cup shredded Parmesan cheese (1 oz)

1½ teaspoons dried basil leaves

1 clove garlic, finely chopped

¼ cup fat-free egg product

12 stone-ground wheat crackers, crushed (about ½ cup)

½ teaspoon pepper

1 cup Italian herb tomato pasta sauce

¼ cup shredded mozzarella cheese (1 oz)

1 Heat oven to 375°F. Spray 13x9-inch (3-quart) glass baking dish with cooking spray. Between sheets of plastic wrap or waxed paper, flatten each chicken breast to ¼-inch thickness (see page 152).

2 In medium bowl, mix spinach, cream cheese, Parmesan cheese, ½ teaspoon of the basil and the garlic until blended. Spread about 1 tablespoon spinach mixture over each chicken breast; roll up tightly. If necessary, secure with toothpicks.

3 Pour egg product into shallow bowl. In another shallow bowl, mix cracker crumbs, pepper and remaining 1 teaspoon basil. Dip each chicken breast into egg product; coat with crumb mixture. Place seam side down in baking dish.

4 Bake uncovered 20 minutes. Pour pasta sauce over chicken; sprinkle with mozzarella cheese. Bake 10 to 15 minutes longer or until chicken is no longer pink in center. Remove toothpicks before serving.

1 Serving: Calories 290; Total Fat 11g (Saturated Fat 4.5g; Trans Fat 0g); Cholesterol 100mg; Sodium 450mg; Total Carbohydrate 10g (Dietary Fiber 2g); Protein 38g **Exchanges:** ½ Starch, 5 Very Lean Meat, 1½ Fat **Carbohydrate Choices:** ½

ultimate chicken fingers

Prep Time: 15 Minutes • **Start to Finish:** 30 Minutes • 4 servings

⅔ cup Original Bisquick™ mix

½ cup grated Parmesan cheese

½ teaspoon salt or garlic salt

½ teaspoon paprika

1 lb boneless skinless chicken breasts, cut crosswise into ½-inch strips

1 egg, slightly beaten

3 tablespoons butter, melted

1 Heat oven to 450°F. Line cookie sheet with foil; spray foil with cooking spray.

2 In 1-gallon resealable food-storage plastic bag, place Bisquick mix, cheese, salt and paprika. Seal bag; shake to mix. Dip half of the chicken strips into beaten egg; add to bag. Seal bag; shake to coat chicken. Place chicken on cookie sheet. Repeat with remaining chicken. Drizzle melted butter over chicken.

3 Bake 12 to 14 minutes, turning once, until chicken is no longer pink in center.

1 Serving: Calories 340; Total Fat 19g (Saturated Fat 9g; Trans Fat 1g); Cholesterol 140mg; Sodium 930mg; Total Carbohydrate 13g (Dietary Fiber 0g); Protein 28g **Exchanges:** 1 Starch, 3½ Very Lean Meat, 3 Fat **Carbohydrate Choices:** 1

Chicken Tenders 6 Ways

Prep Time: 10 Minutes •
Start to Finish: 30 Minutes •
4 servings

* QUICK *

Basic Chicken Tenders

1 package (14 oz) uncooked chicken tenders (not breaded)
1 cup plain panko crispy bread crumbs*
  Flavor Dip (pick your favorite recipe)

1 Heat oven to 400°F. Spray large cookie sheet with cooking spray.

2 In small bowl, mix together Flavor Dip ingredients. Place bread crumbs in large resealable food-storage plastic bag. Place chicken in bread crumb bag; seal and shake to coat. Place chicken on cookie sheet.

3 Bake 15 to 20 minutes, turning once, until chicken is no longer pink in center and bread crumbs are golden brown.

1 Serving (without dip): Calories 230; Total Fat 6g (Saturated Fat 1g; Trans Fat 0g); Cholesterol 60mg; Sodium 105mg; Total Carbohydrate 19g (Dietary Fiber 0g); Protein 24g **Exchanges:** 1 Other carbohydrate, 3½ Very Lean Meat, 1 Fat **Carbohydrate Choices:** 1

Honey-Sriracha Chicken Tenders

FLAVOR DIP

- ¼ cup honey
- ¼ cup Sriracha sauce

SERVE WITH, IF DESIRED

Baked sweet potato fries

Additional Sriracha sauce

1 Serving: Calories 300; Total Fat 6g (Saturated Fat 1g; Trans Fat 0g); Cholesterol 60mg; Sodium 480mg; Total Carbohydrate 37g (Dietary Fiber 0g); Protein 24g **Exchanges:** 1 Starch, 1½ Other Carbohydrate, 3 Very Lean Meat, 1 Fat **Carbohydrate Choices:** 2½

Mango-Chili Chicken Tenders

FLAVOR DIP

- ¼ cup Thai chili garlic paste

MANGO-CHILI SALSA

- 1 cup mango slices, chopped (from 20-oz jar)
- 2 to 3 teaspoons Thai chili garlic paste
- 1 tablespoon chopped fresh cilantro

SERVE WITH, IF DESIRED

Hot cooked jasmine rice

1 While chicken is baking, in medium bowl, mix mango, chili paste and cilantro. Serve with chicken.

1 Serving: Calories 270; Total Fat 6g (Saturated Fat 1g; Trans Fat 0g); Cholesterol 60mg; Sodium 560mg; Total Carbohydrate 28g (Dietary Fiber 0g); Protein 24g **Exchanges:** 1 Starch, 1 Other Carbohydrate, 3 Very Lean Meat, 1 Fat **Carbohydrate Choices:** 2

Honey–Brown Sugar Chicken Tenders

FLAVOR DIP

¼ cup packed dark brown sugar

¼ cup honey

¼ teaspoon salt

SERVE WITH, IF DESIRED

Oven-baked steak fries

Additional honey

1 Serving: Calories 410; Total Fat 11g (Saturated Fat 1.5g; Trans Fat 0g); Cholesterol 60mg; Sodium 270mg; Total Carbohydrate 54g (Dietary Fiber 0g); Protein 24g **Exchanges:** 1 Starch, 2½ Other Carbohydrate, 3 Very Lean Meat, 2 Fat **Carbohydrate Choices:** 3½

Smoky Barbecue Chicken Tenders

FLAVOR DIP

½ cup smoky barbecue sauce

SERVE WITH, IF DESIRED

Corn on the cob

Additional barbecue sauce

1 Serving: Calories 280; Total Fat 6g (Saturated Fat 1g; Trans Fat 0g); Cholesterol 60mg; Sodium 440mg; Total Carbohydrate 32g (Dietary Fiber 0g); Protein 24g **Exchanges:** 1 Starch, 1 Other Carbohydrate, 3 Very Lean Meat, 1 Fat **Carbohydrate Choices:** 2

Pesto Chicken Tenders

FLAVOR DIP

¼ cup basil pesto

2 tablespoons mayonnaise

SERVE WITH, IF DESIRED

Hot cooked pasta tossed with olive oil
and shredded Asiago or Parmesan cheese

1 Serving: Calories 370; Total Fat 24g (Saturated Fat 7g; Trans
Fat 0g); Cholesterol 80mg; Sodium 400mg; Total Carbohydrate
11g (Dietary Fiber 0g); Protein 28g **Exchanges:** ½ Other
Carbohydrate, 3 Very Lean Meat, 1 Medium-Fat Meat, 3½ Fat
Carbohydrate Choices: 1

Ranch Chicken Tenders

FLAVOR DIP

⅓ cup ranch dressing

1 tablespoon chopped fresh basil leaves

SERVE WITH, IF DESIRED

Mashed potatoes

Additional ranch dressing

1 Serving: Calories 320; Total Fat 16g (Saturated Fat 2.5g; Trans
Fat 0g); Cholesterol 70mg; Sodium 320mg; Total Carbohydrate
20g (Dietary Fiber 0g); Protein 24g **Exchanges:** 1 Starch, ½ Other
Carbohydrate, 3 Lean Meat, 1½ Fat **Carbohydrate Choices:** 1

chicken pot pie

Prep Time: 40 Minutes • **Start to Finish:** 1 Hour 15 Minutes • 6 servings

1 box refrigerated pie crusts, softened as directed on box

⅓ cup butter

⅓ cup all-purpose flour

⅓ cup chopped onion

½ teaspoon salt

¼ teaspoon pepper

1¾ cups chicken broth

⅔ cup milk

2½ to 3 cups cut-up cooked chicken

1 box (10 oz) frozen peas and carrots, thawed, drained

1 Heat oven to 425°F. Remove 1 pie crust from pouch; roll into 13-inch square. Ease into ungreased 8-inch square (2-quart) glass baking dish.

2 In 2-quart saucepan, melt butter over medium heat. Stir in flour, onion, salt and pepper. Cook and stir until mixture is bubbly; remove from heat. Stir in broth and milk. Heat to boiling, stirring constantly. Boil and stir 1 minute. Stir in chicken and frozen vegetables. Pour mixture into crust-lined dish.

3 Roll remaining pie crust into 11-inch square. With 1-inch cookie cutter, cut shapes in crust. Place crust over chicken mixture; seal and flute edges. Arrange cutouts on crust.

4 Bake about 35 minutes or until filling is bubbly and crust is golden brown.

1 Serving: Calories 670; Total Fat 43g (Saturated Fat 14g; Trans Fat 5g); Cholesterol 80mg; Sodium 1050mg; Total Carbohydrate 44g (Dietary Fiber 3g); Protein 25g **Exchanges:** 3 Starch, 2½ Lean Meat, 6½ Fat **Carbohydrate Choices:** 3

a new twist

For a chicken divan–style pot pie, substitute 1 box (9 ounces) frozen broccoli cuts, thawed and drained, for the peas and carrots. Stir 1 teaspoon curry powder and a few drops red pepper sauce into flour mixture before cooking. Continue as directed.

easy chicken pot pie

Prep Time: 10 Minutes • **Start to Finish:** 40 Minutes • 4 servings

1 bag (12 oz) frozen mixed vegetables, thawed, drained

1 cup diced cooked chicken

1 can (10¾ oz) condensed cream of chicken soup

1 cup Original Bisquick™ mix

½ cup milk

1 egg

1 Heat oven to 400°F. In ungreased 2-quart casserole, mix vegetables, chicken and soup until blended.

2 In medium bowl, stir Bisquick mix, milk and egg with whisk or fork until blended. Pour over chicken mixture.

3 Bake about 30 minutes or until crust is golden brown.

1 Serving: Calories 360; Total Fat 12g (Saturated Fat 4g; Trans Fat 1.5g); Cholesterol 85mg; Sodium 980mg; Total Carbohydrate 41g (Dietary Fiber 3g); Protein 20g
Exchanges: 1 Starch, 1½ Other Carbohydrate, 1 Vegetable, 2 Very Lean Meat, 2 Fat
Carbohydrate Choices: 3

impossibly easy chicken taco pie

Prep Time: 10 Minutes ● **Start to Finish:** 50 Minutes ● 8 servings

2 cups cut-up cooked chicken

½ cup chopped onion

2 tablespoons taco seasoning mix (from 1-oz package)

1 cup Original Bisquick™ mix

1 cup milk

2 eggs

1 cup shredded Cheddar cheese (4 oz)

Lettuce, if desired

Tomatoes, if desired

Sour Cream, if desired

Cilantro, if desired

1 Heat oven to 400°F. Spray 9-inch glass pie plate with cooking spray.

2 In medium bowl, mix chicken, onion and taco seasoning mix. Sprinkle in pie plate.

3 In same bowl, beat Bisquick mix, milk and eggs with fork until blended. Pour over chicken mixture.

4 Bake 30 to 35 minutes or until knife inserted in center comes out clean. Sprinkle with cheese. Bake 1 to 2 minutes longer or until cheese is melted. Garnish with lettuce, tomatoes, sour cream and cilantro.

1 Serving: Calories 220; Total Fat 10g (Saturated Fat 5g; Trans Fat 0.5g); Cholesterol 95mg; Sodium 490mg; Total Carbohydrate 14g (Dietary Fiber 0g); Protein 18g
Exchanges: 1 Starch, 2 Lean Meat, ½ Fat **Carbohydrate Choices:** 1

make-ahead

This pie can be covered and refrigerated up to 24 hours before baking. You may need to bake a bit longer than the recipe directs since you'll be starting with a cold pie. Watch carefully for doneness.

chicken enchiladas

Prep Time: 25 Minutes • **Start to Finish:** 50 Minutes • 6 servings

1 cup green tomatillo salsa (salsa verde) or salsa

¼ cup cilantro sprigs

¼ cup parsley sprigs

1 tablespoon lime juice

2 cloves garlic

2 cups chopped cooked chicken

¾ cup shredded Monterey Jack cheese (3 oz)

6 flour tortillas (6 to 8 inch)

1 medium lime, cut into wedges

1 Heat oven to 350°F. Spray 11x7-inch (2-quart) glass baking dish with cooking spray.

2 In blender or food processor, place salsa, cilantro, parsley, lime juice and garlic. Cover; blend on high speed about 30 seconds or until smooth.

3 In medium bowl, mix half of the salsa mixture, the chicken and ¼ cup of the cheese. Spoon about ¼ cup chicken mixture down center of each tortilla; roll up. Place seam side down in baking dish. Pour remaining salsa mixture over filled enchiladas. Sprinkle with remaining ½ cup cheese.

4 Bake uncovered 20 to 25 minutes or until hot. Serve with lime wedges.

1 Serving: Calories 300; Total Fat 11g (Saturated Fat 4.5g, Trans Fat 1g); Cholesterol 55mg; Sodium 620mg; Total Carbohydrate 30g (Dietary Fiber 2g); Protein 21g **Exchanges:** 1 Starch, 1 Other Carbohydrate, 2 Lean Meat, ½ High-Fat Meat **Carbohydrate Choices:** 2

cowboy bbq chicken pizza

Prep Time: 10 Minutes • **Start to Finish:** 35 Minutes • 8 servings

2 cups Original Bisquick™ mix

¼ cup sour cream

¼ cup very warm water (120°F to 130°F)

1 container (18 oz) refrigerated original barbecue sauce with shredded chicken

¼ cup chopped packaged precooked bacon (about 4 slices from 2.1-oz package)

1½ cups shredded Colby–Monterey Jack cheese blend (6 oz)

1 Heat oven to 400°F. In medium bowl, stir Bisquick mix, sour cream and warm water with fork until soft dough forms.

2 On surface sprinkled with Bisquick mix, shape dough into a ball; knead 5 times. Roll dough into 14-inch round; fold round in half. Place on ungreased large cookie sheet and unfold.

3 Spread barbecue sauce with chicken over dough to within 2 inches of edge; fold edge just to chicken. Top with half of the bacon. Sprinkle with cheese and remaining bacon.

4 Bake 20 to 25 minutes or until crust is light golden brown and cheese is melted.

1 Serving: Calories 230; Total Fat 14g (Saturated Fat 7g; Trans Fat 1g); Cholesterol 30mg; Sodium 600mg; Total Carbohydrate 19g (Dietary Fiber 0g); Protein 8g **Exchanges:** 2 Starch, 2 Medium-Fat Meat, 2 Fat **Carbohydrate Choices:** 1

swap it out

Precooked bacon is a terrific convenience product and a real time-saver, but you can also cook, drain and chop 4 slices of bacon to use in this recipe.

mexican chicken pizza with cornmeal crust

Prep Time: 20 Minutes • **Start to Finish:** 50 Minutes • 6 servings

1½ cups all-purpose flour

1 tablespoon sugar

1¼ teaspoons regular active dry yeast

¼ teaspoon coarse (kosher or sea) salt

¾ cup warm water (105°F to 115°F)

1 tablespoon olive oil

⅓ cup yellow cornmeal, plus additional for sprinkling

2 cups shredded Mexican cheese blend (8 oz)

1½ cups shredded cooked chicken

1 can (14.5 oz) fire-roasted or plain diced tomatoes, drained

½ medium yellow bell pepper, chopped (½ cup)

¼ cup sliced green onions (4 medium)

¼ cup chopped fresh cilantro

1 Heat oven to 450°F. In medium bowl, mix ¾ cup of the flour, the sugar, yeast and salt. Stir in warm water and oil. Beat with electric mixer on low speed 30 seconds. Beat on high speed 1 minute. Stir in ⅓ cup cornmeal and remaining ¾ cup flour to make a soft dough.

2 On lightly floured surface, knead dough until smooth and elastic, about 5 minutes. Cover; let rest 10 minutes.

3 Spray large cookie sheet with cooking spray; sprinkle with additional cornmeal. On cookie sheet, press dough into 14x10-inch rectangle; prick with fork. Bake 8 to 10 minutes or until edges just begin to turn brown.

4 Sprinkle 1 cup of the cheese over partially baked crust. Top with chicken, tomatoes, bell pepper and remaining 1 cup cheese. Bake 6 to 8 minutes or until cheese is melted and edges are golden brown. Sprinkle with onions and cilantro.

1 Serving: Calories 390; Total Fat 17g (Saturated Fat 8g; Trans Fat 0g); Cholesterol 65mg; Sodium 430mg; Total Carbohydrate 36g (Dietary Fiber 2g); Protein 23g **Exchanges:** 1½ Starch, ½ Other Carbohydrate, 1 Vegetable, 2½ Medium-Fat Meat, 1 Fat **Carbohydrate Choices:** 2½

greek chicken pizza

Prep Time: 15 Minutes • **Start to Finish:** 30 Minutes • 4 servings

1 can (13.8 oz) refrigerated classic pizza crust

1 can (8 oz) pizza sauce

1½ cups shredded mozzarella cheese (6 oz)

2 cups cubed cooked chicken

½ cup thinly sliced red onion

½ cup crumbled feta cheese (2 oz)

¼ cup chopped kalamata olives

1 tablespoon chopped fresh or 1 teaspoon dried oregano leaves

1 Heat oven to 425°F. Spray large cookie sheet with cooking spray. Unroll dough on cookie sheet; starting at center, press dough into 13x9-inch rectangle.

2 Spread pizza sauce over dough to within ½ inch of edges. Top with remaining ingredients.

3 Bake 12 to 15 minutes or until crust is golden brown and cheese is melted.

1 Serving: Calories 610; Total Fat 24g (Saturated Fat 12g; Trans Fat 0.5g); Cholesterol 105mg; Sodium 1410mg; Total Carbohydrate 56g (Dietary Fiber 3g); Protein 44g **Exchanges:** 2½ Starch, 1 Other Carbohydrate, ½ Vegetable, 5 Lean Meat, 1½ Fat **Carbohydrate Choices:** 4

swap it out

Chopped or sliced ripe olives can be substituted for the kalamata olives.

thai chicken pizza

Prep Time: 20 Minutes • **Start to Finish:** 45 Minutes • 6 servings

SAUCE

- ¼ cup reduced-fat (lite) coconut milk (from 14-oz can; not cream of coconut)
- ¼ cup creamy peanut butter
- 1 tablespoon red curry paste
- 1 tablespoon rice vinegar
- 1 tablespoon reduced-sodium soy sauce
- 1 teaspoon finely chopped gingerroot
- 2 cloves garlic, finely chopped

PIZZA

- 1½ cups shredded deli rotisserie chicken
- ¾ cup bite-size strips red bell pepper
- 3 tablespoons honey
- 1½ teaspoons toasted sesame oil
- 1 can (11 oz) refrigerated thin pizza crust
- 1 cup part-skim shredded mozzarella cheese (4 oz)
- 3 tablespoons sliced green onions
- 3 tablespoons chopped roasted peanuts
- 3 tablespoons chopped fresh cilantro

1 Heat oven to 400°F (425°F for shiny pan). Spray dark 15x10x1-inch pan with cooking spray.

2 In small bowl, beat all sauce ingredients with whisk. Set aside.

3 In medium bowl, toss chicken, bell pepper, honey and sesame oil. Set aside.

4 Unroll dough; place in pan. Starting at center, press out dough to edges of pan. Bake about 7 minutes or until edges of crust just begin to turn golden brown. Spread sauce evenly over partially baked crust to within ½ inch of edges. Sprinkle cheese over sauce. Top with chicken mixture.

5 Bake 8 to 12 minutes or until edges are golden brown and cheese is melted. Sprinkle onions, peanuts and cilantro over pizza. Cut and serve immediately.

1 Serving: Calories 420; Total Fat 19g (Saturated Fat 6g; Trans Fat 0g); Cholesterol 40mg; Sodium 790mg; Total Carbohydrate 39g (Dietary Fiber 2g); Protein 24g **Exchanges:** 1 Starch, 1 Other Carbohydrate, ½ Skim Milk, 2 Very Lean Meat, ½ Lean Meat, 3 Fat **Carbohydrate Choices:** 2½

corn-crisped chicken and potato dinner

Prep Time: 20 Minutes • **Start to Finish:** 1 Hour • 4 servings

⅓ cup buttermilk

1 teaspoon salt

¼ teaspoon ground red pepper (cayenne)

⅔ cup corn flake crumbs

4 bone-in chicken breasts (about 2 lb), skin removed

4 medium unpeeled baking potatoes, cut into 1-inch cubes

1 medium red or green bell pepper, cut into 1x½-inch pieces

1 medium onion, cut into 8 wedges

2 tablespoons grated Parmesan cheese

½ teaspoon garlic powder

½ teaspoon paprika

2 tablespoons butter, melted

1 Heat oven to 400°F. Spray 15x10x1-inch pan with cooking spray.

2 In shallow bowl, mix buttermilk, salt and red pepper. Place corn flake crumbs in another shallow bowl. Dip chicken in buttermilk mixture; coat with crumbs. Place chicken in corners of pan.

3 In large bowl, stir together potatoes, bell pepper and onion. Sprinkle with cheese, garlic powder and paprika; toss to coat. Spoon mixture into center of pan. Drizzle melted butter over chicken and vegetables.

4 Bake uncovered 30 to 40 minutes, stirring vegetables once halfway through baking, or until potatoes are tender and juice of chicken is clear when thickest part is cut to bone (at least 165°F).

1 Serving: Calories 480; Total Fat 13g (Saturated Fat 6g, Trans Fat 0g); Cholesterol 120mg; Sodium 860mg; Total Carbohydrate 47g (Dietary Fiber 5g); Protein 44g **Exchanges:** 2½ Starch, ½ Other Carbohydrate, 5 Very Lean Meat, 2 Fat **Carbohydrate Choices:** 3

swap it out

Orange or yellow bell pepper can be substituted for the red or green, or use a combination of colored peppers.

maple-thyme roasted chicken breasts

Prep Time: 20 Minutes • **Start to Finish:** 1 Hour • 4 servings

⅓ cup real maple syrup

2 tablespoons balsamic vinegar

1 tablespoon chopped fresh or 1 teaspoon dried thyme leaves

1 teaspoon salt

1 clove garlic, finely chopped

4 bone-in chicken breasts with large pieces of skin intact (about 3 lb)

4 tablespoons cold butter, each tablespoon cut into smaller pieces

1 tablespoon vegetable oil

¼ teaspoon pepper

1 Heat oven to 425°F. Line 13x9-inch pan with foil.

2 In small bowl, mix maple syrup, vinegar, thyme, ½ teaspoon of the salt and the garlic.

3 Starting on one side of each chicken breast, slowly work your fingers under the skin. (You are trying to loosen the connection between the skin and meat, not remove the skin.) Place chicken skin side up in pan. Drizzle about 2 tablespoons syrup mixture under the skin of each chicken breast, spreading evenly over meat. Dot each with 1 tablespoon butter pieces. Replace any skin you may have displaced. Rub skin with oil; sprinkle with pepper and remaining ½ teaspoon salt.

4 Roast uncovered 30 to 35 minutes or until juice of chicken is clear when thickest part is cut to bone (at least 165°F). Let stand 5 minutes before serving.

1 Serving: Calories 530; Total Fat 28g (Saturated Fat 10g; Trans Fat 1g); Cholesterol 165mg; Sodium 780mg; Total Carbohydrate 19g (Dietary Fiber 0g); Protein 50g **Exchanges:** 1½ Other Carbohydrate, 7 Lean Meat, 1 Fat **Carbohydrate Choices:** 1

soy–brown sugar–glazed chicken thighs

Prep Time: 15 Minutes • **Start to Finish:** 40 Minutes • 4 servings

¼ cup packed brown sugar
¼ cup soy sauce
1 tablespoon rice vinegar
½ teaspoon ground ginger
1 clove garlic, finely chopped
1½ lb skin-on bone-in chicken thighs
1 tablespoon vegetable oil

1 Heat oven to 375°F. In small bowl, beat brown sugar, soy sauce, vinegar, ginger and garlic with whisk until well combined. Set aside.

2 Heat 10-inch ovenproof skillet or roasting pan over medium-high heat. Rub chicken with oil; place skin side down in skillet. Cook chicken, without moving, 3 to 5 minutes or until skin is browned and chicken releases easily from skillet.

3 Transfer chicken to plate. Pour off drippings from skillet. Return chicken to skillet, skin side up. Pour brown sugar–soy mixture over chicken.

4 Roast 15 to 25 minutes or until juice of chicken is clear when thickest part is cut to bone (at least 165°F). Serve chicken with sauce.

1 Serving: Calories 330; Total Fat 17g (Saturated Fat 4g; Trans Fat 0g); Cholesterol 90mg; Sodium 1000mg; Total Carbohydrate 15g (Dietary Fiber 0g); Protein 30g **Exchanges:** 1 Other Carbohydrate, 4 Lean Meat, 1 Fat **Carbohydrate Choices:** 1

swap it out

To avoid the cutting board entirely, use preminced garlic, or substitute ½ teaspoon garlic powder for the fresh garlic.

honey-baked sriracha chicken wings

Prep Time: 20 Minutes • **Start to Finish:** 1 Hour 10 Minutes • 12 servings (about 2 wings each)

CHICKEN

- 2 tablespoons Sriracha sauce
- 1 tablespoon vegetable oil
- ½ teaspoon salt
- ½ teaspoon freshly ground pepper
- 3 lb chicken wing drummettes
- ½ cup all-purpose flour

GLAZE

- ¼ cup honey
- 2 tablespoons apricot jam
- 2 tablespoons Sriracha sauce
- 1 tablespoon soy sauce
- 2 teaspoons lime juice
- 3 cloves garlic, finely chopped

1 Heat oven to 425°F. Line 2 cookie sheets with sides with heavy-duty foil; spray foil with cooking spray.

2 In 1-gallon resealable food-storage plastic bag, mix Sriracha sauce, oil, salt, pepper and drummettes. Seal bag; shake to coat. Add flour; seal bag, and shake until drummettes are coated with flour. Place drummettes on cookie sheets.

3 Bake uncovered 30 minutes. Turn drummettes over, and rotate cookie sheets. Bake 20 to 30 minutes longer or until golden brown and juice of drummettes is clear when thickest part is cut to bone (at least 165°F).

4 Meanwhile, in 1-quart saucepan, mix all glaze ingredients. Heat to simmering over medium heat, stirring frequently, until slightly thickened, about 5 minutes. Remove from heat; set aside.

5 In large bowl, toss drummettes with sauce. Serve warm.

1 Serving: Calories 180; Total Fat 9g (Saturated Fat 2.5g; Trans Fat 0g); Cholesterol 35mg; Sodium 310mg; Total Carbohydrate 14g (Dietary Fiber 0g); Protein 11g **Exchanges:** 1 Other Carbohydrate, 1½ Medium-Fat Meat **Carbohydrate Choices:** 1

buffalo chicken wings

Prep Time: 20 Minutes • **Start to Finish:** 55 Minutes • 12 servings (2 wings each)

12 chicken wings
   (about 2 lb)

 2 tablespoons butter

½ cup all-purpose flour

½ teaspoon salt

¼ teaspoon pepper

 1 cup barbecue sauce

 1 tablespoon red
   pepper sauce

½ teaspoon
   Cajun seasoning

¼ teaspoon ground cumin

 1 bottle (8 oz) blue cheese
   dressing, if desired

   Celery, carrot and
   zucchini sticks, if desired

1 Heat oven to 425°F. Cut each chicken wing at joints to make 3 pieces; discard tip. Cut off and discard excess skin.

2 In 13x9-inch pan, melt butter in oven. In 1-gallon resealable food-storage plastic bag, mix flour, salt and pepper. Add chicken; seal bag tightly. Shake until chicken is completely coated with flour mixture. Place chicken in pan.

3 Bake uncovered 20 minutes. In small bowl, mix barbecue sauce, pepper sauce, Cajun seasoning and cumin. Turn chicken. Pour sauce mixture over chicken; toss until evenly coated with sauce. Bake 10 to 12 minutes longer or until light golden brown on outside and no longer pink in center.

4 Serve chicken wings with dressing and vegetables.

1 Serving: Calories 110; Total Fat 3.5g (Saturated Fat 1.5g; Trans Fat 0g); Cholesterol 20mg; Sodium 430mg; Total Carbohydrate 13g (Dietary Fiber 0g); Protein 6g **Exchanges:** 1 Other Carbohydrate, 1 Lean Meat **Carbohydrate Choices:** 1

sticky ginger-garlic chicken wings

Prep Time: 20 Minutes • **Start to Finish:** 1 Hour 20 Minutes • 30 servings (about 2 wings each)

GLAZE

- ½ cup packed brown sugar
- ½ cup rice vinegar
- 2 tablespoons grated gingerroot
- 1 tablespoon Sriracha sauce or ½ teaspoon crushed red pepper flakes
- 3 cloves garlic, finely chopped
- 1 teaspoon soy sauce

CHICKEN

- 3 tablespoons red pepper sauce
- 2 tablespoons vegetable oil
- ½ teaspoon salt
- ½ teaspoon pepper
- 5 lb chicken wing drummettes
- 1 cup all-purpose flour

1 Heat oven to 375°F. Line 2 two 15x10x1-oven pans with heavy-duty foil; spray foil with cooking spray.

2 In 1-quart saucepan, stir together all glaze ingredients. Heat to simmering over medium heat, stirring frequently, until sugar is dissolved, about 5 minutes. Remove from heat; set aside.

3 In 2-gallon resealable food-storage plastic bag, mix pepper sauce, oil, salt, pepper and chicken. Seal bag; shake to coat. Add flour; seal bag and shake until chicken is coated with flour. Place chicken on cookie sheets.

4 Bake 30 minutes. Turn chicken over and rotate cookie sheets. Bake 20 to 30 minutes longer or until golden brown on outside and no longer pink in center.

5 In large bowl, toss chicken with glaze.

1 Serving: Calories 70; Total Fat 2.5g (Saturated Fat 0.5g; Trans Fat 0g); Cholesterol 15mg; Sodium 110mg; Total Carbohydrate 7g (Dietary Fiber 0g); Protein 5g **Exchanges:** ½ Other Carbohydrate, ½ Lean Meat **Carbohydrate Choices:** ½

CHAPTER 3

Easy Stove-Top

buttermilk fried chicken sandwiches with spicy slaw

Prep Time: 30 Minutes • **Start to Finish:** 40 Minutes • 4 sandwiches

SLAW

- ¼ cup mayonnaise
- ¼ cup sour cream
- 4 to 5 teaspoons Sriracha sauce
- 1 cup thinly sliced green cabbage
- 1 cup thinly sliced red cabbage
- 1 tablespoon finely chopped red onion

CHICKEN

- 4 boneless skinless chicken breasts (about 1¼ lb)
- ½ cup all-purpose flour
- ½ teaspoon salt
- ½ teaspoon pepper
- ½ teaspoon paprika
- 1 cup buttermilk
- 1 cup vegetable oil
- 4 burger buns or ciabatta rolls, split, toasted

1 In medium bowl, mix mayonnaise, sour cream and Sriracha sauce until well blended. Remove ¼ cup to small bowl; cover and refrigerate until serving time. Add cabbage and onion to bowl with remaining mayonnaise mixture; toss to coat. Cover and refrigerate.

2 Between sheets of plastic wrap or waxed paper, flatten each chicken breast to ¼-inch thickness (see page 152). In shallow dish, mix flour, salt, pepper and paprika. Pour buttermilk into another shallow dish. Coat chicken with flour mixture, shaking off excess. Dip into buttermilk, allowing excess to drip back into dish. Coat again in flour mixture, shaking off excess.

3 In 10-inch skillet, heat oil over medium-high heat. Cook chicken in oil 6 to 8 minutes, turning once, until no longer pink in center and coating is golden brown. Remove chicken from pan with slotted spoon or spatula; place on paper towels.

4 Spread cut sides of buns with reserved mayonnaise mixture. On each bun bottom, place 1 chicken breast; top with slaw. Cover with bun tops.

1 Sandwich: Calories 480; Total Fat 25g (Saturated Fat 6g; Trans Fat 0g); Cholesterol 120mg; Sodium 680mg; Total Carbohydrate 22g (Dietary Fiber 1g); Protein 42g **Exchanges:** ½ Starch, 1 Other Carbohydrate, ½ Vegetable, 5½ Lean Meat, 1½ Fat **Carbohydrate Choices:** 1½

make-ahead

The day before serving, slice the cabbage and chop the onion, and place in a resealable food-storage plastic bag. Prepare the chicken as directed in step 2, and place in a resealable food-storage plastic bag. Refrigerate until ready to cook.

fried chicken and waffle sandwich bites

Prep Time: 1 Hour 30 Minutes • **Start to Finish:** 1 Hour 30 Minutes • 16 sandwich bites

BACON

8 slices bacon, cut in half

FRIED CHICKEN

2 boneless skinless chicken breasts (4 oz each)

⅛ teaspoon salt

Dash black pepper

½ cup Original Bisquick™ mix

½ teaspoon chipotle chile powder

1 egg

2 tablespoons vegetable oil

BUTTER

¼ cup butter, softened

2 tablespoons real maple syrup

2 teaspoons bourbon whiskey

WAFFLES

1¼ cups Original Bisquick™ mix

1 egg

¾ cup regular or nonalcoholic beer (6 oz)

1 tablespoon vegetable oil

1 In 12-inch skillet, cook bacon over low heat 8 to 10 minutes, turning occasionally, until crisp. Drain on paper towels. Set aside.

2 Between pieces of plastic wrap or waxed paper, flatten each chicken breast to ½-inch thickness (see page 152). Cut into 2-inch pieces. Sprinkle chicken with salt and pepper.

3 In shallow bowl, mix ½ cup Bisquick mix and the chipotle powder. In another shallow bowl, beat egg with fork. Dip chicken into egg mixture; coat with Bisquick mix mixture.

4 In 12-inch nonstick skillet, heat 2 tablespoons oil over medium heat. Add chicken; cook 6 to 8 minutes, turning once, until chicken is no longer pink in center and coating is golden brown. Meanwhile, in another small bowl, stir maple-bourbon butter ingredients until smooth. Set aside.

5 Heat waffle maker. In medium bowl, stir all waffle ingredients until blended. Pour about 1 tablespoon batter onto center of each quarter of hot waffle maker. Close lid of waffle maker. Bake about 2 minutes or until steaming stops. Carefully remove waffles. Repeat with remaining batter, making 32 small waffles.

6 To assemble: Place waffle section on plate; spread maple-bourbon butter on waffle, top with 1 half slice bacon, 1 piece chicken, and another waffle section.

1 Sandwich Bite: Calories 160; Total Fat 10g (Saturated Fat 3.5g; Trans Fat 0.5g); Cholesterol 45mg; Sodium 320mg; Total Carbohydrate 11g (Dietary Fiber 0g); Protein 6g **Exchanges:** ½ Starch, ½ Lean Meat, 2 Fat **Carbohydrate Choices:** 1

moroccan spiced chicken

Prep Time: 30 Minutes • **Start to Finish:** 30 Minutes • 4 servings

1 tablespoon paprika

½ teaspoon salt

½ teaspoon ground cumin

¼ teaspoon ground allspice

¼ teaspoon ground cinnamon

4 boneless skinless chicken breasts (about 1¼ lb)

1 tablespoon vegetable oil

2 cups water

1 teaspoon vegetable oil

1½ cups uncooked couscous

¼ cup raisins, if desired

1 small papaya, peeled, seeded and sliced

1 In small bowl, mix paprika, salt, cumin, allspice and cinnamon. Rub spice mixture on both sides of chicken.

2 In 10-inch skillet, heat 1 tablespoon oil over medium heat. Cook chicken in oil 15 to 20 minutes, turning once, until juice of chicken is clear when center of thickest part is cut (at least 165°F).

3 Meanwhile, in 2-quart saucepan, heat water and 1 teaspoon oil just to boiling. Stir in couscous; remove from heat. Cover; let stand 5 minutes. Fluff couscous; stir in raisins. Serve chicken with couscous and papaya.

1 Serving: Calories 470; Total Fat 10g (Saturated Fat 2g; Trans Fat 0g); Cholesterol 85mg; Sodium 380mg; Total Carbohydrate 55g (Dietary Fiber 5g); Protein 40g **Exchanges:** 3½ Starch, 4½ Very Lean Meat, 1 Fat **Carbohydrate Choices:** 3½

indian spiced chicken and chutney

Prep Time: 25 Minutes • **Start to Finish:** 1 Hour 25 Minutes • 4 servings

MARINADE

- ½ cup plain yogurt
- 1 tablespoon lemon juice
- 2 teaspoons grated gingerroot
- ½ teaspoon paprika
- ½ teaspoon ground coriander
- ½ teaspoon salt
- ¼ teaspoon ground red pepper (cayenne)
- ⅛ teaspoon ground cloves

CHICKEN AND CHUTNEY

- 4 boneless skinless chicken breasts (about 1¼ lb)
- ½ cup mango chutney
- Hot cooked basmati rice or regular long-grain white rice, if desired

1 In small bowl, mix all marinade ingredients. Place chicken in resealable food-storage plastic bag or shallow glass or plastic dish. Pour marinade over chicken; turn to coat. Seal bag or cover dish; refrigerate 1 hour.

2 In 12-inch skillet, cook chicken and marinade over medium-high heat 15 to 20 minutes, turning once, until juice of chicken is clear when center of thickest part is cut (at least 165°F).

3 Spoon chutney over chicken. Serve with rice.

1 Serving: Calories 230; Total Fat 5g (Saturated Fat 1.5g; Trans Fat 0g); Cholesterol 85mg; Sodium 410mg; Total Carbohydrate 13g (Dietary Fiber 0g); Protein 33g **Exchanges:** 1 Fruit, 4½ Very Lean Meat, ½ Fat **Carbohydrate Choices:** 1

chicken korma

Prep Time: 30 Minutes • **Start to Finish:** 1 Hour 30 Minutes • 4 servings

1 lb boneless skinless chicken breasts, cut crosswise into ½-inch strips

¼ cup whipping cream

2 tablespoons finely chopped gingerroot

5 cloves garlic, finely chopped

1 tablespoon finely chopped fresh cilantro

1 teaspoon coriander seed, crushed

½ teaspoon cumin seed, crushed

½ teaspoon salt

¼ teaspoon ground red pepper (cayenne)

2 tablespoons butter

½ cup tomato sauce

¼ cup finely chopped fresh or 2 tablespoons crumbled dried fenugreek leaves

1 In medium bowl, mix all ingredients except butter, tomato sauce and fenugreek. Cover; refrigerate at least 1 hour but no longer than 24 hours.

2 In 10-inch skillet, melt butter over medium heat. Add chicken mixture and tomato sauce. Cook about 5 minutes, stirring frequently, until chicken is partially cooked.

3 Stir in fenugreek; reduce heat. Cover; simmer about 10 minutes longer or until chicken is no longer pink in center.

1 Serving: Calories 270; Total Fat 15g (Saturated Fat 8g; Trans Fat 0g); Cholesterol 100mg; Sodium 570mg; Total Carbohydrate 7g (Dietary Fiber 2g); Protein 28g
Exchanges: ½ Starch, 3½ Lean Meat, 1 Fat **Carbohydrate Choices:** ½

swap it out

Watercress leaves or fresh parsley can be substituted for the fenugreek, but the flavor will be milder.

crunchy cornmeal chicken with mango-peach salsa

Prep Time: 30 Minutes • **Start to Finish:** 30 Minutes • 4 servings

CHICKEN

- ½ cup yellow cornmeal
- ½ teaspoon salt
- ¼ teaspoon pepper
- 4 boneless skinless chicken breasts (about 1¼ lb)
- 2 tablespoons vegetable oil

SALSA

- 3 medium peaches, peeled, chopped (1½ cups)
- 1 ripe large mango, seed removed, peeled and chopped (1½ cups)
- 1 large tomato, seeded, chopped (1 cup)
- ¼ cup chopped fresh cilantro
- 3 tablespoons vegetable oil
- 2 tablespoons white vinegar
- ¼ teaspoon salt

1 In shallow dish, mix cornmeal, ½ teaspoon salt and the pepper. Coat chicken with cornmeal mixture.

2 In 10-inch skillet, heat 2 tablespoons oil over medium-high heat. Cook chicken in oil 15 to 20 minutes, turning once, until juice of chicken is clear when center of thickest part is cut (at least 165°F).

3 Meanwhile, in large bowl, mix all salsa ingredients. Serve chicken with salsa.

1 Serving: Calories 450; Total Fat 22g (Saturated Fat 4g; Trans Fat 0g); Cholesterol 85mg; Sodium 520mg; Total Carbohydrate 30g (Dietary Fiber 5g); Protein 34g **Exchanges:** 2 Fruit, 5 Lean Meat, 1 Fat **Carbohydrate Choices:** 2

swap it out

Refrigerated mango slices (from a jar), well drained, can be substituted for the fresh mango. And 1½ cups chopped frozen (thawed) sliced peaches can be substituted for the fresh peaches.

southwestern chicken scaloppine

Prep Time: 30 Minutes   •   **Start to Finish:** 30 Minutes   •   4 servings

4   boneless skinless chicken breasts (about 1¼ lb)

¼   cup all-purpose flour

1   teaspoon ground cumin

½   teaspoon salt

2   tablespoons vegetable oil

½   cup chicken broth

¼   teaspoon red pepper sauce, if desired

2   tablespoons lime juice

2   tablespoons chopped fresh cilantro

1 Between sheets of plastic wrap or waxed paper, flatten each chicken breast to ¼-inch thickness (see page 152). Cut chicken into smaller pieces, if desired.

2 In shallow dish, mix flour, cumin and salt. Reserve 1 teaspoon flour mixture. Coat chicken with remaining flour mixture.

3 In 12-inch nonstick skillet, heat oil over medium heat. Add chicken; cook 6 to 10 minutes, turning once, until golden brown and no longer pink in center. Remove chicken from skillet; cover to keep warm.

4 In small bowl, stir reserved 1 teaspoon flour mixture into broth. Gradually stir broth mixture and pepper sauce into skillet. Heat to boiling; stir in lime juice and cilantro. Serve sauce over chicken.

1 Serving: Calories 260; Total Fat 12g (Saturated Fat 2.5g; Trans Fat 0g); Cholesterol 85mg; Sodium 500mg; Total Carbohydrate 7g (Dietary Fiber 0g); Protein 33g
Exchanges: ½ Other Carbohydrate, 4½ Very Lean Meat, 2 Fat **Carbohydrate Choices:** ½

coffee chicken with quick mole sauce

Prep Time: 45 Minutes • **Start to Finish:** 2 Hours 45 Minutes • 6 servings

CHICKEN AND MARINADE

- 4 cups water
- ⅓ cup salt
- ⅓ cup packed dark brown sugar
- 1 tablespoon cumin seed
- 1 tablespoon chili powder
- 1 lime, thinly sliced
- 1 cup strong brewed coffee
- 6 boneless skinless chicken breasts (about 1¾ lb)
- 2 tablespoons vegetable oil

SAUCE

- 1 medium onion, thinly sliced
- 2 cloves garlic, finely chopped
- 1 can (28 oz) crushed tomatoes, undrained
- 1¼ cups chicken broth
- 1 tablespoon creamy peanut butter
- 1 teaspoon sugar
- ½ teaspoon ground cumin

  Dash ground cinnamon
- 1 oz unsweetened baking chocolate
- 2 chipotle chiles in adobo sauce, chopped

1 In 2-quart saucepan, heat water, salt, brown sugar, cumin seed, chili powder and lime slices over medium heat, stirring occasionally, until salt and brown sugar are dissolved. Remove from heat; stir in coffee. Cool to room temperature.

2 Place chicken in 1-gallon resealable food-storage plastic bag or large bowl; pour cooled coffee mixture over chicken. Seal bag or cover bowl; refrigerate 2 to 3 hours.

3 Remove chicken from marinade; discard marinade. Pat chicken dry with paper towels. In 12-inch skillet, heat oil over medium heat. Cook chicken in oil 5 to 6 minutes, turning once, until golden brown. Remove from skillet; set aside.

4 Add onion to skillet; cook over medium heat 5 minutes, stirring occasionally, until soft and lightly browned. Add garlic; cook 30 seconds or until fragrant. Add remaining sauce ingredients. Cook uncovered 3 minutes, stirring occasionally, until mixture simmers and peanut butter and chocolate are melted.

5 Reduce heat to medium-low; arrange chicken in sauce. Cook uncovered 15 to 20 minutes, stirring occasionally, until sauce thickens and juice of chicken is clear when center of thickest part is cut (at least 165°F).

1 Serving: Calories 320; Total Fat 14g (Saturated Fat 4g; Trans Fat 0g); Cholesterol 80mg; Sodium 2130mg; Total Carbohydrate 15g (Dietary Fiber 3g); Protein 33g **Exchanges:** ½ Starch, ½ Other Carbohydrate, 4½ Lean Meat **Carbohydrate Choices:** 1

spicy skillet chicken

Prep Time: 25 Minutes • **Start to Finish:** 25 Minutes • 4 servings

1 to 2 teaspoons chili powder

½ teaspoon salt

¼ teaspoon pepper

4 boneless skinless chicken breasts (about 1¼ lb)

1 tablespoon vegetable oil

1 can (15 oz) black beans, drained, rinsed

1 can (11 oz) whole kernel corn with red and green peppers, undrained

⅓ cup chunky-style salsa

2 cups hot cooked rice

1 In small bowl, mix chili powder, salt and pepper. Sprinkle evenly over both sides of chicken breasts.

2 In 10-inch nonstick skillet, heat oil over medium heat. Add chicken; cook 8 to 10 minutes, turning once, until juice of chicken is clear when center of thickest part is cut (at least 165°F).

3 Stir in beans, corn and salsa. Heat to boiling. Reduce heat. Cover and simmer 3 to 5 minutes or until vegetables are hot. Serve with rice.

1 Serving: Calories 510; Total Fat 9g (Saturated Fat 2g; Trans Fat 0g); Cholesterol 85mg; Sodium 1070mg; Total Carbohydrate 63g (Dietary Fiber 11g); Protein 43g **Exchanges:** 3½ Starch, ½ Other Carbohydrate, 4½ Very Lean Meat, 1 Fat **Carbohydrate Choices:** 4

thai-style coconut chicken

Prep Time: 25 Minutes • **Start to Finish:** 25 Minutes • 4 servings

1 tablespoon vegetable oil

1 lb boneless skinless chicken breasts, cut into bite-size pieces

1 teaspoon grated lime peel

1 teaspoon grated gingerroot

1 clove garlic, finely chopped

2 serrano chiles or 1 jalapeño chile, seeded, finely chopped

¼ cup finely chopped fresh cilantro

1 can (14 oz) coconut milk (not cream of coconut)

1 teaspoon packed brown sugar

½ teaspoon salt

1 tablespoon soy sauce

1 cup fresh sugar snap peas

1 medium green bell pepper, cut into 1-inch pieces

1 medium tomato, seeded, chopped (¾ cup)

1 tablespoon chopped fresh basil leaves

Hot cooked jasmine rice, if desired

1 In 12-inch nonstick skillet or wok, heat oil over medium-high heat. Cook chicken in oil 2 to 3 minutes, stirring constantly, until no longer pink in center. Add lime peel, gingerroot, garlic, chiles and cilantro; cook and stir 1 minute.

2 Pour coconut milk over chicken. Stir in brown sugar, salt, soy sauce, peas and bell pepper. Reduce heat to medium. Simmer uncovered 3 to 5 minutes, stirring occasionally, until vegetables are crisp-tender. Stir in tomato.

3 Spoon chicken mixture into shallow serving bowls; top with basil. Serve with rice.

1 Serving: Calories 430; Total Fat 26g (Saturated Fat 17g; Trans Fat 0g); Cholesterol 85mg; Sodium 650mg; Total Carbohydrate 14g (Dietary Fiber 4g); Protein 35g
Exchanges: ½ Starch, 1 Vegetable, 5 Lean Meat, 2 Fat **Carbohydrate Choices:** 1

cashew chicken and broccoli

Prep Time: 30 Minutes • **Start to Finish:** 30 Minutes • 4 servings

2 teaspoons oil

1 lb boneless skinless chicken breasts, cut into 1-inch pieces

1 teaspoon finely chopped gingerroot

2 cups fresh broccoli florets

1 cup reduced-sodium chicken broth

⅛ teaspoon crushed red pepper flakes

2 cups frozen sugar snap peas (from 12-oz bag)

3 tablespoons reduced-sodium soy sauce

2 teaspoons rice vinegar

1 tablespoon cornstarch

1 teaspoon sugar

2 medium green onions, sliced (2 tablespoons)

3 cups hot cooked brown rice

¼ cup salted roasted cashew halves and pieces

1 In 12-inch nonstick skillet or wok, heat oil over medium-high heat. Cook chicken and gingerroot in oil 4 to 5 minutes, stirring constantly, until chicken begins to brown.

2 Add broccoli, ½ cup of the broth and the pepper flakes. Cover; cook over medium heat 2 minutes, stirring once. Add peas; cook 2 to 4 minutes longer, stirring once, until vegetables are crisp-tender.

3 In small bowl, mix remaining ½ cup broth, the soy sauce, vinegar, cornstarch and sugar; stir into chicken mixture. Add onions; cook and stir until sauce is thickened and bubbly.

4 Serve chicken mixture over rice. Sprinkle with cashews.

1 Serving: Calories 440; Total Fat 11g (Saturated Fat 2g; Trans Fat 0g); Cholesterol 70mg; Sodium 660mg; Total Carbohydrate 51g (Dietary Fiber 8g); Protein 35g **Exchanges:** 2½ Starch, 3 Vegetable, 3 Lean Meat **Carbohydrate Choices:** 3½

swap it out

Frozen broccoli florets can be substituted for the fresh.

pan-fried chicken with romesco sauce

Prep Time: 20 Minutes • **Start to Finish:** 40 Minutes • 6 servings

SAUCE

- ½ cup slivered almonds
- 1 slice firm crusty white bread (about 5x5x½ inch)
- 1 medium tomato, cut in half, seeded
- 2 cloves garlic, peeled
- 1 jar (12 oz) roasted red bell peppers, rinsed, drained and patted dry
- ¼ cup olive oil
- 1 tablespoon sherry vinegar
- ½ teaspoon salt
- ¼ teaspoon smoked paprika

CHICKEN

- 2 tablespoons olive oil
- 6 boneless skinless chicken breasts (about 1¾ lb)
- 1 teaspoon garlic salt
- Chopped fresh parsley, if desired

1 Heat oven to 400°F. In 15x10x1-inch pan, place almonds, bread, tomato and garlic in single layer. Bake 5 to 6 minutes or until almonds and bread are lightly toasted. Break bread into bite-size pieces.

2 In food processor, place toasted almonds, bread, tomato and garlic. Cover; process, using quick on-and-off motions, until coarsely chopped. Add remaining sauce ingredients. Cover; process, using quick on-and-off motions, until almost smooth. Transfer sauce to small bowl; set aside. Sauce will thicken as it stands.

3 In 12-inch nonstick skillet, heat 2 tablespoons oil over medium heat. Sprinkle both sides of chicken with garlic salt; add to skillet. Cook 15 to 20 minutes, turning once, until juice of chicken is clear when center of thickest part is cut (at least 165°F). Serve chicken with sauce. Sprinkle with parsley.

1 Serving: Calories 400; Total Fat 23g (Saturated Fat 4g; Trans Fat 0g); Cholesterol 105mg; Sodium 630mg; Total Carbohydrate 8g (Dietary Fiber 1g); Protein 39g **Exchanges:** ½ Other Carbohydrate, 5½ Very Lean Meat, 4 Fat **Carbohydrate Choices:** ½

make-ahead

The sauce can be made up to 1 day ahead; cover and refrigerate. Let stand at room temperature 30 minutes before serving.

swap it out

If you can't find sherry vinegar, use red wine vinegar instead.

extra-creamy basil chicken

Prep Time: 10 Minutes • **Start to Finish:** 30 Minutes • 4 servings

1 package (3 oz) cream cheese, softened

⅓ cup Italian dressing

1 pouch (9 oz) creamy parmesan-basil cooking sauce

1 tablespoon vegetable oil

4 boneless skinless chicken breasts (about 1¼ lb)

½ teaspoon salt

½ teaspoon pepper

1 In medium bowl, mix cream cheese, Italian dressing and cooking sauce until smooth.

2 In 12-inch skillet, heat oil over medium-low heat. Add chicken to skillet; sprinkle with salt and pepper. Cook chicken 5 to 7 minutes on each side or until juice of chicken is clear when center of thickest part is cut (at least 165°F).

3 Stir in cooking sauce mixture. Heat to boiling; reduce heat. Simmer uncovered about 15 minutes, stirring occasionally, until mixture starts to thicken.

1 Serving: Calories 370; Total Fat 24g (Saturated Fat 8g; Trans Fat 0.5g); Cholesterol 100mg; Sodium 760mg; Total Carbohydrate 8g (Dietary Fiber 0g); Protein 30g
Exchanges: ½ Starch, 4 Very Lean Meat, 4½ Fat **Carbohydrate Choices:** ½

basil and prosciutto chicken

Prep Time: 25 Minutes • **Start to Finish:** 25 Minutes • 4 servings

1 tablespoon vegetable oil

4 boneless skinless chicken breasts (about 1¼ lb)

4 teaspoons Dijon mustard

4 thin slices prosciutto or cooked ham

¼ cup shredded mozzarella cheese (1 oz)

4 large fresh basil leaves

1 In 10-inch skillet, heat oil over medium heat. Add chicken; cook 6 minutes. Turn chicken; brush with mustard and top with prosciutto. Cook 6 to 8 minutes longer or until juice of chicken is clear when center of thickest part is cut (at least 165°F).

2 Sprinkle cheese over chicken. Cook about 2 minutes longer or until cheese is melted. Garnish with basil.

1 Serving: Calories 260; Total Fat 11g (Saturated Fat 3g, Trans Fat 0g); Cholesterol 110mg; Sodium 300mg; Total Carbohydrate 0g (Dietary Fiber 0g); Protein 40g **Exchanges:** 5½ Very Lean Meat, 1½ Fat **Carbohydrate Choices:** 0

chicken saltimbocca

Prep Time: 30 Minutes ▪ **Start to Finish:** 30 Minutes ▪ 4 servings

4 boneless skinless chicken breasts (1¼ to 1½ lb)

⅓ cup all-purpose flour

2 tablespoons grated Parmesan cheese

1 teaspoon Italian seasoning

½ teaspoon salt

2 tablespoons olive or vegetable oil

4 thin slices prosciutto or cooked ham

4 slices (1 oz each) mozzarella cheese

1 teaspoon chopped fresh sage leaves

¾ cup chicken broth

1 tablespoon butter

1 Between sheets of plastic wrap or waxed paper, flatten each chicken breast to ¼-inch thickness (see page 152). In shallow dish, mix flour, Parmesan cheese, Italian seasoning and salt. Coat chicken with flour mixture; shake off excess.

2 In 12-inch nonstick skillet, heat oil over medium-high heat. Add chicken; cook about 8 minutes, turning once, until browned on outside and no longer pink in center.

3 Top each chicken breast with 1 slice prosciutto and 1 slice mozzarella cheese. Cover skillet tightly; cook 1 to 2 minutes or until cheese is melted. Sprinkle sage over chicken. Remove chicken from skillet to serving platter. Cover loosely with tent of foil, being careful not to let foil touch cheese.

4 Add broth to skillet. Increase heat to high. Heat to boiling, scraping up any browned bits from bottom of skillet. Boil about 3 minutes or until broth is reduced to about ¼ cup. Remove from heat; stir in butter. Spoon over chicken.

1 Serving: Calories 460; Total Fat 24g (Saturated Fat 9g; Trans Fat 0g); Cholesterol 140mg; Sodium 1130mg; Total Carbohydrate 9g (Dietary Fiber 0g); Protein 52g
Exchanges: ½ Starch, 7 Lean Meat, ½ Fat **Carbohydrate Choices:** ½

chicken marsala

Prep Time: 35 Minutes • **Start to Finish:** 35 Minutes • 4 servings

4 boneless skinless chicken breasts (about 1¼ lb)

½ cup all-purpose flour

¼ teaspoon salt

¼ teaspoon pepper

2 tablespoons olive or vegetable oil

2 cloves garlic, finely chopped

1 cup sliced fresh mushrooms (3 oz)

¼ cup chopped fresh parsley or 1 tablespoon parsley flakes

½ cup Marsala wine or chicken broth

Hot cooked pasta, if desired

1 Between sheets of plastic wrap or waxed paper, flatten each chicken breast to ¼-inch thickness (see page 152). In shallow dish, mix flour, salt and pepper. Coat chicken with flour mixture.

2 In 10-inch skillet, heat oil over medium-high heat. Cook garlic, mushrooms and parsley in oil 5 minutes, stirring frequently.

3 Add chicken to skillet. Cook about 8 minutes, turning once, until browned. Add wine. Cook 8 to 10 minutes longer or until chicken is no longer pink in center. Serve with pasta.

1 Serving: Calories 280; Total Fat 8g (Saturated Fat 2g; Trans Fat 0g); Cholesterol 85mg; Sodium 230mg; Total Carbohydrate 17g (Dietary Fiber 0g); Protein 34g **Exchanges:** 1 Starch, 4 Very Lean Meat, 1 Fat **Carbohydrate Choices:** 1

chicken piccata

Prep Time: 25 Minutes • **Start to Finish:** 25 Minutes • 6 servings

6 boneless skinless chicken breasts (about 1½ lb)

1 egg

1 tablespoon water

½ cup seasoned dry bread crumbs

½ teaspoon salt

¼ teaspoon pepper

⅛ teaspoon garlic powder

¼ cup all-purpose flour

2 tablespoons butter

2 tablespoons vegetable oil

2 tablespoons lemon juice

2 tablespoons dry white wine or chicken broth

Chopped fresh parsley, if desired

Lemon wedges, if desired

1 Between sheets of plastic wrap or waxed paper, flatten each chicken breast to ¼-inch thickness (see below). In small bowl, beat egg and water. In shallow bowl, mix bread crumbs, salt, pepper and garlic powder. Coat chicken with flour. Dip into egg mixture; coat with crumb mixture.

2 In 12-inch skillet, heat butter and oil over medium heat. Add chicken; cook 8 to 10 minutes, turning once, until no longer pink in center. Remove chicken from skillet; keep warm.

3 Stir lemon juice and wine into drippings in skillet. Heat to boiling; pour over chicken. Sprinkle with parsley. Serve with lemon wedges.

1 Serving: Calories 290; Total Fat 14g (Saturated Fat 4.5g; Trans Fat 0g); Cholesterol 115mg; Sodium 370mg; Total Carbohydrate 11g (Dietary Fiber 0g); Protein 28g
Exchanges: ½ Starch, 4 Very Lean Meat, 2½ Fat **Carbohydrate Choices:** 1

Flattening Chicken Breasts

Place chicken breast between pieces of plastic wrap or waxed paper. Using flat side of meat mallet or rolling pin, pound from center out, until ¼ inch thick.

Or, using the heel of your hand, apply firm pressure to chicken breasts (pounding lightly if necessary), pressing until ¼ inch thick.

Simple Side Dishes

If you often find yourself stumped on side dishes and you don't want your basic veggies, potatoes, rice or pasta, explore these sides. No more boring in your bowl or on your plate!

Kale with Sriracha-Honey Butter: Mix together equal amounts of honey, melted butter and a few drops Sriracha sauce. Toss with hot cooked baby kale leaves. Sprinkle with honey-roasted peanuts.

Bacon-Cheddar Brussels Sprouts: Toss hot cooked Brussels sprouts with bacon drippings, olive oil or melted butter. Top with shredded Cheddar cheese and crumbled bacon.

Green Beans with Gorgonzola and Toasted Pecans: Top hot cooked whole green beans with crumbled Gorgonzola or blue cheese and toasted pecan halves. Add a few twists of freshly ground pepper.

Beet Caprese: On individual salad plates, alternate slices of cooked beets and slices of fresh mozzarella cheese. Drizzle lightly with olive oil, sprinkle with coarse sea salt and freshly ground coarse black pepper. Top with sliced fresh basil leaves.

Alfredo Mashed Potatoes with French-Fried Onions: Substitute jarred or refrigerated Alfredo sauce for the milk and butter when making mashed potatoes. Top with canned French-fried onions.

Easy Bacon-Cheese Fries: Make your favorite frozen type of French fries as directed on package. Place in shallow serving platter. Drizzle any flavor hot process cheese sauce or salsa con queso dip over fries. Sprinkle with cooked bacon bits and sliced green onions.

Pesto Pasta Toss: Toss hot cooked pasta with basil pesto; heat gently if necessary. Sprinkle with shredded, shaved or grated Parmesan cheese.

Salsa Rice: Stir salsa and sliced ripe olives into hot cooked rice; heat gently if necessary. Sprinkle with shredded taco-flavored cheese or Cheddar cheese.

tuscan rosemary chicken and white beans

Prep Time: 30 Minutes   •   **Start to Finish:** 30 Minutes   •   4 servings

⅓ cup Italian dressing

4 boneless skinless chicken breasts (about 1¼ lb)

¼ cup water

2 medium carrots, thinly sliced (1 cup)

2 medium stalks celery, sliced (1 cup)

¼ cup coarsely chopped drained sun-dried tomatoes in oil

1 teaspoon dried rosemary leaves, crushed

1 can (19 oz) cannellini beans, drained, rinsed

1 In 12-inch skillet, heat dressing over medium-high heat. Add chicken; cook 4 to 6 minutes, turning once, until lightly browned.

2 Reduce heat to medium-low. Add water, carrots, celery, tomatoes and rosemary. Cover; simmer about 10 minutes or until carrots are crisp-tender and juice of chicken is clear when center of thickest part is cut (at least 165°F).

3 Stir in beans. Cover; cook 5 to 6 minutes or until beans are thoroughly heated.

1 Serving: Calories 390; Total Fat 9g (Saturated Fat 2g; Trans Fat 0g); Cholesterol 85mg; Sodium 340mg; Total Carbohydrate 33g (Dietary Fiber 8g); Protein 42g **Exchanges:** 1½ Starch, ½ Other Carbohydrate, 5½ Very Lean Meat, 1 Fat **Carbohydrate Choices:** 2

swap it out

Substitute 8 boneless skinless chicken thighs for the chicken breasts.

chicken milanese

Prep Time: 25 Minutes • **Start to Finish:** 25 Minutes • 4 servings

CHICKEN

- 4 boneless skinless chicken breasts (about 1¼ lb)
- ¾ cup Italian-style bread crumbs
- ¼ cup freshly grated Parmesan cheese (1 oz)
- ⅛ teaspoon pepper
- ⅓ cup all-purpose flour
- 2 eggs, lightly beaten
- 1 tablespoon olive or vegetable oil

SALAD

- 2 tablespoons olive or vegetable oil
- 1 teaspoon lemon juice
- ¼ teaspoon salt
- ¼ teaspoon coarsely ground pepper
- 4 cups arugula or mixed greens

SAUCE AND PARMESAN

- 1 cup tomato pasta sauce, heated
- ½ cup shaved Parmesan cheese

1 Cut chicken breasts in half horizontally to make 8 thin pieces.

2 In medium bowl, mix bread crumbs, ¼ cup grated Parmesan cheese and ⅛ teaspoon pepper; set aside. In separate medium shallow bowls, place flour and eggs.

3 Coat chicken with flour, shaking off excess, then dip into eggs, letting any excess drip back into bowl. Coat chicken with bread crumb mixture, pressing to coat.

4 In 12-inch nonstick skillet, heat 1 tablespoon oil over medium-high heat. Add chicken; cook about 2 minutes or until golden on bottom. Turn chicken over; cook 3 to 4 minutes longer or until golden on outside and no longer pink in center.

5 In small bowl, beat all salad ingredients except arugula with whisk. In medium bowl, toss arugula with oil mixture to coat.

6 Place 2 chicken pieces in center of each of 4 plates. Spoon about ¼ cup of the pasta sauce around chicken on each plate. Spoon salad on top of chicken. Top with shaved Parmesan cheese.

1 Serving: Calories 560; Total Fat 26g (Saturated Fat 7g, Trans Fat 0g); Cholesterol 205mg; Sodium 1210mg; Total Carbohydrate 36g (Dietary Fiber 2g); Protein 46g **Exchanges:** 1½ Starch, 1 Other Carbohydrate, 6 Very Lean Meat, 4 Fat **Carbohydrate Choices:** 2½

chicken with mushrooms and carrots

Prep Time: 35 Minutes • **Start to Finish:** 35 Minutes • 4 servings

4 slices bacon, chopped

4 boneless skinless chicken breasts (about 1¼ lb)

¼ teaspoon pepper

2 cups ready-to-eat baby-cut carrots

1 cup chicken broth

¼ cup dry white wine or chicken broth

1 tablespoon cornstarch

½ teaspoon dried thyme leaves

¼ teaspoon salt

4 oz small fresh mushrooms, cut in half (about 1⅓ cups)

1 In 12-inch nonstick skillet, cook bacon over medium heat 6 to 8 minutes, stirring occasionally, until crisp. Drain bacon on paper towels.

2 Add chicken to bacon drippings in skillet; sprinkle with pepper. Cook over medium heat 4 to 5 minutes, turning once, until well browned. Add carrots and ¼ cup of the broth. Cover; cook 7 to 9 minutes or until carrots are crisp-tender and juice of chicken is clear when center of thickest part is cut (at least 165°F).

3 In small bowl, mix wine, cornstarch, thyme, salt and remaining ¾ cup broth. Add broth mixture and mushrooms to skillet. Cook 3 to 5 minutes, stirring once or twice, until bubbly. Cover; cook about 3 minutes longer or until mushrooms are tender. Sprinkle with bacon.

1 Serving: Calories 260; Total Fat 8g (Saturated Fat 2.5g; Trans Fat 0g); Cholesterol 95mg; Sodium 710mg; Total Carbohydrate 9g (Dietary Fiber 2g); Protein 37g **Exchanges:** ½ Other Carbohydrate, 1 Vegetable, 5 Very Lean Meat, 1 Fat **Carbohydrate Choices:** ½

chicken with chipotle alfredo sauce

Prep Time: 30 Minutes • **Start to Finish:** 30 Minutes • 4 servings

2 cups uncooked penne pasta (6 oz)

1 tablespoon olive oil

1 lb boneless skinless chicken breasts, cut into ½-inch pieces

2 cloves garlic, finely chopped

1 chipotle chile in adobo sauce (from 7-oz can), finely chopped

1 jar (16 oz) Alfredo pasta sauce

2 tablespoons chopped fresh cilantro

1 Cook and drain pasta as directed on package.

2 Meanwhile, in 10-inch skillet, heat oil over medium-high heat. Cook chicken and garlic in oil 5 to 7 minutes, stirring occasionally, until chicken is no longer pink in center. Stir in chile and Alfredo sauce; cook 2 minutes longer, stirring frequently.

3 Serve chicken mixture over pasta. Sprinkle with cilantro.

1 Serving: Calories 740; Total Fat 44g (Saturated Fat 24g, Trans Fat 1.5g); Cholesterol 185mg; Sodium 530mg; Total Carbohydrate 45g (Dietary Fiber 2g); Protein 41g
Exchanges: 3 Starch, 4½ Lean Meat, 6 Fat **Carbohydrate Choices:** 3

chicken carbonara deluxe

Prep Time: 10 Minutes • **Start to Finish:** 30 Minutes • 4 servings

1 package (7 oz)
   uncooked spaghetti

8 slices bacon, cut into
   ½-inch pieces

1 medium onion, chopped
   (½ cup)

1 clove garlic,
   finely chopped

2 cups cut-up
   cooked chicken

½ cup grated
   Parmesan cheese

½ cup whipping cream

1 Cook and drain spaghetti as directed on package.

2 Meanwhile, cook bacon in 3-quart saucepan over low heat 8 to 10 minutes, stirring frequently, until crisp. Remove bacon from saucepan with slotted spoon; drain. Drain drippings from saucepan, reserving 1 tablespoon in saucepan.

3 Cook onion and garlic in bacon drippings over medium heat about 3 minutes, stirring frequently, until onion is tender. Stir in spaghetti, chicken, cheese and whipping cream. Cook, stirring occasionally, until heated through. Toss with bacon.

1 Serving: Calories 590; Total Fat 28g (Saturated Fat 13g, Trans Fat 0.5g); Cholesterol 130mg; Sodium 950mg; Total Carbohydrate 47g (Dietary Fiber 3g); Protein 39g **Exchanges:** 1½ Starch, 1½ Other Carbohydrate, 3 Very Lean Meat, 1 Lean Meat, 1 High-Fat Meat, 3 Fat **Carbohydrate Choices:** 3

swap it out

Try pancetta instead of bacon. Pancetta, a cured meat, is imported from Italy and is similar to bacon.

pesto ravioli with chicken

Prep Time: 25 Minutes • **Start to Finish:** 25 Minutes • 4 servings

2 teaspoons olive or vegetable oil

1 lb uncooked chicken breast tenders (not breaded)

¾ cup chicken broth

1 package (9 oz) refrigerated cheese-filled ravioli

3 small zucchini, cut into ¼-inch slices

1 large red bell pepper, thinly sliced

¼ cup basil pesto

Freshly grated Parmesan cheese, if desired

1 In 12-inch skillet, heat oil over medium-high heat. Cook chicken in oil about 4 minutes, turning occasionally, until browned. Remove chicken from skillet; set aside.

2 Add broth and ravioli to skillet. Heat to boiling; reduce heat. Cover; simmer about 4 minutes or until ravioli is tender.

3 Stir in zucchini, bell pepper and chicken. Cook over medium-high heat about 3 minutes, stirring occasionally, until vegetables are crisp-tender and chicken is no longer pink in center. Add pesto; toss to coat. Sprinkle with cheese.

1 Serving: Calories 440; Total Fat 18g (Saturated Fat 6g; Trans Fat 0g); Cholesterol 85mg; Sodium 660mg; Total Carbohydrate 34g (Dietary Fiber 3g); Protein 36g **Exchanges:** 1½ Starch, ½ Other Carbohydrate, 1 Vegetable, 4 Lean Meat, 1 Fat **Carbohydrate Choices:** 2

bow ties with chicken and asparagus

Prep Time: 25 Minutes • **Start to Finish:** 25 Minutes • 6 servings (1½ cups each)

4 cups uncooked bow-tie (farfalle) pasta (8 oz)

1 lb fresh asparagus spears

1 tablespoon canola oil

1 lb boneless skinless chicken breasts, cut into 1-inch pieces

1 package (8 oz) sliced fresh mushrooms (3 cups)

2 cloves garlic, finely chopped

1 cup chicken broth

1 tablespoon cornstarch

4 medium green onions, sliced (¼ cup)

2 tablespoons chopped fresh basil leaves

Salt, if desired

¼ cup finely shredded Parmesan cheese (1 oz)

1 Cook and drain pasta as directed on package, omitting salt.

2 Meanwhile, break off tough ends of asparagus as far down as stalks snap easily. Wash asparagus; cut into 1-inch pieces.

3 In 12-inch nonstick skillet, heat oil over medium-high heat. Add chicken; cook 2 minutes, stirring occasionally. Stir in asparagus, mushrooms and garlic. Cook 6 to 8 minutes, stirring occasionally, until chicken is no longer pink in center and vegetables are tender.

4 In small bowl, gradually stir broth into cornstarch. Stir in onions and basil. Stir cornstarch mixture into chicken mixture. Cook and stir 1 to 2 minutes or until thickened and bubbly. Season with salt. Toss with pasta. Sprinkle with cheese.

1 Serving: Calories 320; Total Fat 7g (Saturated Fat 2g; Trans Fat 0g); Cholesterol 50mg; Sodium 210mg; Total Carbohydrate 37g (Dietary Fiber 3g); Protein 27g **Exchanges:** 2 Starch, 1 Vegetable, 2½ Very Lean Meat, 1 Fat **Carbohydrate Choices:** 2½

skillet chicken nachos

Prep Time: 20 Minutes • **Start to Finish:** 20 Minutes • 6 servings

1 tablespoon olive or vegetable oil

1¼ lb boneless skinless chicken breasts, cut into ¼-inch pieces

1 package (1 oz) taco seasoning mix

1 can (8 oz) tomato sauce

1 medium red bell pepper, chopped (1 cup)

1 can (15 oz) black beans, drained, rinsed

1 can (7 oz) whole kernel sweet corn, drained

2 cups shredded Mexican cheese blend (8 oz)

6 oz tortilla chips (about 42 chips)

¼ cup chopped fresh cilantro

1 In 12-inch nonstick skillet, heat oil over medium-high heat. Cook chicken in oil 3 to 5 minutes, stirring occasionally, until no longer pink in center.

2 Stir in taco seasoning mix, tomato sauce, bell pepper, beans, corn and 1 cup of the cheese. Reduce heat to medium; cook 3 to 5 minutes, stirring occasionally, until hot and cheese is melted.

3 Divide tortilla chips among 6 plates. Spoon chicken mixture evenly over chips. Sprinkle with remaining 1 cup cheese and the cilantro.

1 Serving: Calories 520; Total Fat 24g (Saturated Fat 9g; Trans Fat 0g); Cholesterol 95mg; Sodium 1320mg; Total Carbohydrate 38g (Dietary Fiber 5g); Protein 36g **Exchanges:** 2 Starch, ½ Other Carbohydrate, ½ Vegetable, 4 Very Lean Meat, 4 Fat **Carbohydrate Choices:** 2½

swap it out

Shredded pepper Jack cheese can be substituted for the Mexican cheese blend.

spicy peanut chicken

Prep Time: 25 Minutes • **Start to Finish:** 25 Minutes • 4 servings

¼ cup chicken broth

1 tablespoon cornstarch

1 tablespoon sugar

2 tablespoons soy sauce

1 tablespoon white vinegar

¼ teaspoon ground red pepper (cayenne)

1 tablespoon vegetable oil

1 lb boneless skinless chicken thighs or breasts, cut into ¾-inch pieces

1 clove garlic, finely chopped

1 teaspoon grated gingerroot

1 medium red bell pepper, cut into ¾-inch pieces

⅓ cup dry-roasted peanuts

2 medium green onions, sliced (2 tablespoons)

1 In small bowl, mix broth, cornstarch, sugar, soy sauce, vinegar and red pepper; set aside.

2 Heat 12-inch skillet or wok over high heat. Add oil; rotate wok to coat side. Add chicken, garlic and gingerroot; cook about 3 minutes, stirring constantly, until chicken is no longer pink in center. Add bell pepper; cook and stir 1 minute.

3 Add broth mixture to wok. Cook and stir about 1 minute or until sauce is thickened. Stir in peanuts. Sprinkle with onions.

1 Serving: Calories 250; Total Fat 14g (Saturated Fat 2.5g; Trans Fat 0g); Cholesterol 50mg; Sodium 590mg; Total Carbohydrate 11g (Dietary Fiber 2g); Protein 20g
Exchanges: ½ Other Carbohydrate, ½ Vegetable, 2½ Medium-Fat Meat, ½ Fat
Carbohydrate Choices: 1

caramel chicken with pickled cucumber and onion

Prep Time: 25 Minutes • **Start to Finish:** 50 Minutes • 4 servings

PICKLED CUCUMBER AND ONION

¼ cup cider vinegar

1 teaspoon granulated sugar

¼ teaspoon crushed red pepper flakes

¼ teaspoon salt

⅛ teaspoon pepper

1 medium cucumber

1 small red onion, cut in half, sliced (½ cup)

CHICKEN AND SAUCE

½ cup packed brown sugar

⅔ cup chicken broth

3 tablespoons rice vinegar

2 tablespoons soy sauce

1 tablespoon vegetable oil

8 boneless skinless chicken thighs, cut into 1-inch pieces

1 teaspoon finely chopped gingerroot

2 cloves garlic, finely chopped

Hot cooked rice, if desired

Black sesame seed or toasted sesame seed, if desired

1 In medium glass or plastic bowl, mix cider vinegar, granulated sugar, pepper flakes, salt and pepper until sugar is dissolved. Cut cucumber in half lengthwise; remove seeds with spoon. Cut each half crosswise into ¼-inch slices. Add cucumber and onion to bowl; toss to coat. Set aside; stir occasionally.

2 In small bowl, mix brown sugar, broth, rice vinegar and soy sauce until sugar is almost dissolved; set aside. In 12-inch nonstick skillet, heat oil over medium-high heat. Add chicken, gingerroot and garlic; cook about 5 minutes, stirring occasionally, until chicken is lightly browned.

3 Add broth mixture to skillet. Heat to boiling; reduce heat to medium-low. Cook uncovered 20 to 25 minutes or until chicken is golden brown and sauce is thickened and reduced by half.

4 Serve chicken and sauce over rice. Top with pickled cucumber and onion. Sprinkle with sesame seed.

1 Serving: Calories 430; Total Fat 14g (Saturated Fat 3.5g; Trans Fat 0g); Cholesterol 120mg; Sodium 860mg; Total Carbohydrate 33g (Dietary Fiber 1g); Protein 42g **Exchanges:** 2 Other Carbohydrate, 6 Very Lean Meat, 2 Fat **Carbohydrate Choices:** 2

make-ahead

Make the cucumber mixture up to 1 day ahead. Refrigerate until serving time.

swap it out

If you don't have rice vinegar, you can use cider vinegar in the sauce.

skillet chicken thighs with bacon and spinach

Prep Time: 40 Minutes • **Start to Finish:** 40 Minutes • 4 servings

8 boneless skinless chicken thighs (1½ to 1¾ lb)

3 slices bacon, chopped

2 large carrots, chopped (1½ cups)

2 small onions, sliced

3 cloves garlic, finely chopped

½ cup chicken broth

1 bag (8 oz) fresh baby spinach leaves (6 cups)

½ teaspoon salt

¼ teaspoon pepper

1 tablespoon chopped fresh or ½ teaspoon dried sage leaves

1 tablespoon grated lemon peel

1 In 12-inch skillet, cook chicken and bacon over medium-high heat 5 minutes, turning chicken once.

2 Stir in carrots, onions, garlic and broth. Cook uncovered 15 to 20 minutes, turning chicken and stirring frequently, until juice of chicken is clear when center of thickest part is cut (at least 165°F) and vegetables are tender.

3 Remove from heat; add spinach, salt and pepper. Stir mixture about 3 minutes or until spinach wilts. Stir in sage and lemon peel until well blended.

1 Serving: Calories 350; Total Fat 16g (Saturated Fat 5g; Trans Fat 0g); Cholesterol 110mg; Sodium 720mg; Total Carbohydrate 11g (Dietary Fiber 3g); Protein 40g **Exchanges:** 1½ Vegetable, 5½ Lean Meat **Carbohydrate Choices:** 1

beer-braised chicken

Prep Time: 35 Minutes • **Start to Finish:** 1 Hour 25 Minutes • 4 servings

2 tablespoons butter

1 large onion, cut in half, thinly sliced (1 cup)

4 bone-in chicken thighs, skin removed

4 chicken drumsticks, skin removed

¾ teaspoon salt

¼ teaspoon pepper

¾ cup stout or dark beer

2 tablespoons all-purpose flour

1 In 12-inch skillet, melt butter over medium-high heat. Cook onion in butter 3 to 5 minutes, stirring occasionally, until crisp-tender. Sprinkle all sides of chicken with salt and pepper. Add chicken to skillet; cook 4 to 6 minutes, turning once, until browned.

2 Pour beer around chicken. Heat to boiling; reduce heat to low. Cover; simmer 45 to 50 minutes or until juice of chicken is clear when thickest part is cut to bone (at least 165°F). Remove chicken from skillet; cover to keep warm.

3 In small bowl, mix flour and ¼ cup hot cooking juices with whisk until smooth. Pour mixture into skillet; cook over medium heat 5 to 6 minutes, stirring constantly with whisk, until thickened and bubbly. Serve chicken with gravy.

1 Serving: Calories 300; Total Fat 13g (Saturated Fat 6g; Trans Fat 0g); Cholesterol 130mg; Sodium 600mg; Total Carbohydrate 8g (Dietary Fiber 0g); Protein 36g
Exchanges: ½ Other Carbohydrate, 5 Very Lean Meat, 2½ Fat **Carbohydrate Choices:** ½

swap it out

If you don't like beer, substitute dry white wine or chicken broth instead.

chicken tagine

Prep Time: 30 Minutes • **Start to Finish:** 1 Hour • 6 servings

1 tablespoon olive or vegetable oil

1 cut-up whole chicken (3 to 3½ lb)

1 medium onion, sliced

2 cloves garlic, finely chopped

¼ cup chopped fresh cilantro

1 teaspoon ground cumin

1 teaspoon ground turmeric

1 teaspoon ground ginger

1 teaspoon salt

1 cinnamon stick (2 inch)

1 cup chicken broth

1 can (14.5 oz) diced tomatoes, undrained

1 cup pitted dried plums, cut into bite-size pieces

½ cup pitted green olives

1 small lemon, cut into quarters

Hot cooked couscous or rice, if desired

Chopped fresh cilantro, if desired

1 In 4-quart Dutch oven or saucepan, heat oil over medium-high heat. Place chicken skin side down in hot oil; add onion and garlic. Cook uncovered 6 to 10 minutes, turning occasionally, until chicken is browned on all sides.

2 Reduce heat to medium. Sprinkle cilantro, cumin, turmeric, ginger and salt over chicken. Add cinnamon stick; pour broth and tomatoes over chicken. Turn chicken several times to coat evenly. Add plums, olives and lemon, pressing into liquid around chicken. Reduce heat to low. Cover; simmer about 30 minutes or until juice of chicken is clear when thickest pieces are cut to bone (at least 165°F).

3 Place chicken on deep serving platter; cover to keep warm. Increase heat to high; boil sauce uncovered about 5 minutes, stirring occasionally, until thickened. Pour sauce over chicken. Serve over couscous. Garnish with additional chopped fresh cilantro.

1 Serving: Calories 370; Total Fat 18g (Saturated Fat 4.5g; Trans Fat 0g); Cholesterol 85mg; Sodium 920mg; Total Carbohydrate 23g (Dietary Fiber 4g); Protein 29g **Exchanges:** ½ Fruit, 2 Vegetable, 3½ Medium-Fat Meat, ½ Fat **Carbohydrate Choices:** 1½

coq au vin

Prep Time: 45 Minutes • **Start to Finish:** 1 Hour 20 Minutes • 6 servings

½ cup all-purpose flour

1½ teaspoons salt

¼ teaspoon pepper

1 cut-up whole chicken
(3 to 3½ lb)

8 slices bacon

¾ cup frozen small whole
onions (from 1-lb bag)

1 package (8 oz) sliced
fresh mushrooms (about
3 cups)

1 cup chicken broth

1 cup dry red wine or
nonalcoholic red wine

4 medium carrots, cut into
2-inch pieces

1 clove garlic,
finely chopped

Bouquet garni*

1 In shallow dish, mix flour, 1 teaspoon of the salt and the pepper. Coat chicken with flour mixture.

2 In 12-inch skillet, cook bacon over medium heat 8 to 10 minutes, turning once, until crisp. Drain bacon on paper towels. Crumble bacon; set aside. Add chicken to bacon drippings in skillet; cook over medium heat about 15 minutes, turning occasionally, until browned on all sides.

3 Move chicken to one side of skillet; add onions and mushrooms to other side. Cook uncovered over medium-high heat about 6 minutes, stirring occasionally, until mushrooms are tender; drain.

4 Add bacon, broth, wine, carrots, garlic, the remaining ½ teaspoon salt and the bouquet garni to skillet. Heat to boiling; reduce heat. Cover; simmer about 35 minutes or until juice of chicken is clear when thickest pieces are cut to bone (at least 165°F). Remove and discard bouquet garni; skim off excess fat.

Slow Cooker Directions: Remove skin from chicken. Decrease flour to ⅓ cup. Cut carrots into ½-inch pieces. Cook, drain and crumble bacon; refrigerate. Brown chicken as directed. Spray 3½- to 6-quart slow cooker with cooking spray. In slow cooker, place carrots and chicken. Mix all remaining ingredients except mushrooms and bacon; pour over chicken. Cover; cook on Low heat setting 4 to 6 hours. Stir in mushrooms and bacon. Increase heat setting to High. Cover; cook 30 minutes longer. Remove bouquet garni; skim off excess fat.

✳ Tie ½ teaspoon dried thyme leaves, 2 large sprigs fresh parsley and 1 dried bay leaf in cheesecloth bag, or place in tea ball.

1 Serving: Calories 350; Total Fat 19g (Saturated Fat 6g; Trans Fat 0g); Cholesterol 95mg; Sodium 1020mg; Total Carbohydrate 12g (Dietary Fiber 1g); Protein 33g **Exchanges:** 1 Starch, 2 Vegetable, 4 Lean Meat, ½ Fat **Carbohydrate Choices:** 1

chicken cacciatore

Prep Time: 40 Minutes • **Start to Finish:** 1 Hour 20 Minutes • 6 servings

1 cut-up whole chicken (3 to 3½ lb)

½ cup all-purpose flour

¼ cup vegetable oil

2 medium onions

1 medium green bell pepper

1 can (14.5 oz) diced tomatoes, undrained

1 can (8 oz) tomato sauce

1 cup sliced fresh mushrooms (3 oz)

1½ teaspoons chopped fresh or ½ teaspoon dried oregano leaves

1 teaspoon chopped fresh or ¼ teaspoon dried basil leaves

½ teaspoon salt

2 cloves garlic, finely chopped

Hot cooked pasta, if desired

Grated Parmesan cheese, if desired

1 Coat chicken with flour. In 12-inch skillet, heat oil over medium-high heat. Cook chicken in oil 15 to 20 minutes or until browned on all sides; drain.

2 Cut onions and bell pepper in half; cut each half crosswise into quarters. Add onions, bell pepper and all remaining ingredients except pasta and cheese to skillet with chicken; stir.

3 Heat to boiling; reduce heat. Cover; simmer 30 to 40 minutes or until juice of chicken is clear when thickest pieces are cut to bone (at least 165°F). Serve with pasta; sprinkle with cheese.

1 Serving: Calories 400; Total Fat 23g (Saturated Fat 5g; Trans Fat 0g); Cholesterol 85mg; Sodium 630mg; Total Carbohydrate 19g (Dietary Fiber 3g); Protein 30g **Exchanges:** 3 Vegetable, 3 Medium-Fat Meat, 2 Fat **Carbohydrate Choices:** 1

chicken and dumplings

Prep Time: 20 Minutes • **Start to Finish:** 3 Hours • 4 servings

1 cut-up whole chicken (3 to 3½ lb)

4 medium stalks celery (with leaves), chopped (about 2 cups)

1 large onion, chopped (1 cup)

1 medium carrot, sliced (½ cup)

¼ cup chopped fresh parsley or 1 tablespoon parsley flakes

1½ teaspoons salt

⅛ teaspoon pepper

5 cups water

2 cups all-purpose flour

1 tablespoon parsley flakes, if desired

2 teaspoons baking powder

3 tablespoons cold butter or shortening

¾ cup milk

1 Remove excess fat from chicken. In 4-quart Dutch oven or saucepan, place chicken, celery, onion, carrot, fresh parsley, 1 teaspoon of the salt, the pepper and water. Heat to boiling; reduce heat. Cover; simmer about 2 hours or until juice of chicken is clear when thickest pieces are cut to bone (at least 165°F).

2 Remove chicken and vegetables from Dutch oven. Skim ½ cup fat from broth; reserve. Transfer broth to large bowl; reserve 4 cups. (Save remaining broth for another use.)

3 In Dutch oven or stockpot, heat reserved ½ cup fat over low heat. Stir in ½ cup of the flour. Cook and stir until mixture is smooth and bubbly; remove from heat. Stir in reserved 4 cups broth. Heat to boiling, stirring constantly. Boil and stir 1 minute. Add chicken and vegetables; reduce heat to low. Cook about 20 minutes or until hot.

4 In medium bowl, mix remaining 1½ cups flour, remaining ½ teaspoon salt, the parsley flakes and baking powder. Cut in butter, using pastry blender or fork, until mixture looks like fine crumbs. Stir in milk. Drop dough by spoonfuls onto hot chicken mixture (do not drop directly into liquid or dumplings may become soggy). Cook uncovered over low heat 10 minutes. Cover; cook 10 minutes longer.

1 Serving: Calories 820; Total Fat 55g (Saturated Fat 16g; Trans Fat 2.5g); Cholesterol 120mg; Sodium 1770mg; Total Carbohydrate 48g (Dietary Fiber 1g); Protein 34g **Exchanges:** 3 Starch, 3½ Medium-Fat Meat, 6 Fat **Carbohydrate Choices:** 3

a new twist

For a quicker version of the recipe, omit all dumpling ingredients in step 4. In step 3, stir in ½ cup Original Bisquick mix instead of the flour. Continue as directed in step 3. In step 4, in medium bowl, stir 2 cups Bisquick mix and ⅔ cup milk with fork or whisk until soft dough forms. Drop dough by spoonfuls and cook as directed.

skillet-fried chicken

Prep Time: 20 Minutes • **Start to Finish:** 40 Minutes • 6 servings

½ cup all-purpose flour

1 tablespoon paprika

1½ teaspoons salt

½ teaspoon pepper

1 cut-up whole chicken
(3 to 3½ b)

Vegetable oil

1 In shallow dish, mix flour, paprika, salt and pepper. Coat chicken with flour mixture.

2 In 12-inch nonstick skillet, heat ¼ inch oil over medium-high heat. Add chicken skin side down. Cook about 10 minutes or until light brown on all sides; reduce heat to low. Turn chicken skin side up.

3 Simmer uncovered about 20 minutes, without turning, until juice of chicken is clear when thickest pieces are cut to bone (at least 165°F).

1 Serving: Calories 330; Total Fat 20g (Saturated Fat 4.5g; Trans Fat 0g); Cholesterol 85mg; Sodium 670mg; Total Carbohydrate 9g (Dietary Fiber 0g); Protein 28g
Exchanges: ½ Starch, 4 Medium-Fat Meat **Carbohydrate Choices:** ½

a new twist

To make a buttermilk version of the chicken, increase flour to 1 cup. Dip chicken into 1 cup buttermilk before coating with flour mixture.

chicken à la king

Prep Time: 25 Minutes • **Start to Finish:** 25 Minutes • 6 servings (1½ cups each)

½   cup butter

1   small green bell pepper, chopped (½ cup)

1   cup sliced fresh mushrooms (3 oz)

½   cup all-purpose flour

½   teaspoon salt

¼   teaspoon pepper

1½ cups milk

1¼ cups chicken broth

2   cups cut-up cooked chicken

1   jar (2 oz) diced pimientos, drained

Toasted baguette slices or hot cooked rice, if desired

1 In 3-quart saucepan, melt butter over medium-high heat. Cook bell pepper and mushrooms in butter, stirring occasionally, until bell pepper is crisp-tender.

2 Stir in flour, salt and pepper. Cook and stir over medium heat until bubbly; remove from heat.

3 Stir in milk and broth. Heat to boiling, stirring constantly. Boil and stir 1 minute. Stir in chicken and pimientos; cook until hot. Serve over baguette slices.

1 Serving: Calories 300; Total Fat 20g (Saturated Fat 11g; Trans Fat 1g); Cholesterol 85mg; Sodium 580mg; Total Carbohydrate 12g (Dietary Fiber 0g); Protein 17g **Exchanges:** 1 Starch, 2 Lean Meat, 2½ Fat **Carbohydrate Choices:** 1

a new twist

For a turkey version of à la king, substitute 2 cups cut-up cooked turkey for the chicken.

swap it out

You can use a 4-ounce can of mushrooms pieces and stems instead of the fresh mushrooms. Drain the liquid, or add it with the milk in step 2 for a mightier mushroom flavor.

bbq chicken fajitas

Prep Time: 30 Minutes • **Start to Finish:** 30 Minutes • 5 servings (2 fajitas each)

1 package (1 oz) fajita seasoning mix

1 large red bell pepper, cut into thin strips

1 large green bell pepper, cut into thin strips

1 large onion, cut in half lengthwise and sliced

1 tablespoon vegetable oil

2 cups cut-up shredded deli rotisserie chicken

½ cup barbecue sauce

10 flour tortillas for soft tacos and fajitas (6 inch), heated as directed on package

1 Place fajita seasoning mix in gallon-size resealable food-storage plastic bag. Place vegetables in bag; seal. Shake vegetables until evenly coated.

2 In 12-inch nonstick skillet, heat oil over medium-high heat. Add vegetables; cook and stir, scraping any seasoning mix from bottom of skillet, 3 to 4 minutes or until vegetables are almost crisp-tender. Stir in chicken and barbecue sauce. Cook and stir 2 to 3 minutes longer or until chicken and sauce are heated through.

3 Spoon about ½ cup chicken mixture down center of each tortilla; fold in one end and roll up.

1 Serving: Calories 370; Total Fat 11g (Saturated Fat 2.5g; Trans Fat 1.5g); Cholesterol 50mg; Sodium 1320mg; Total Carbohydrate 46g (Dietary Fiber 3g); Protein 20g **Exchanges:** 1½ Starch, 1½ Other Carbohydrate, ½ Vegetable, 1 Very Lean Meat, 1 Lean Meat, 1½ Fat **Carbohydrate Choices:** 3

pulled chicken sandwiches with root beer barbecue sauce

Prep Time: 40 Minutes • **Start to Finish:** 40 Minutes • 4 sandwiches

SAUCE

- ½ cup root beer
- ½ cup ketchup
- 3 tablespoons cider vinegar
- 2 tablespoons yellow mustard
- 1 tablespoon packed brown sugar
- 2 teaspoons Worcestershire sauce
- ¼ teaspoon salt
- ¼ teaspoon pepper
- ⅛ teaspoon ground ginger
- 1 clove garlic, crushed

  Dash red pepper sauce

SANDWICHES

- 3 cups shredded deli rotisserie chicken (from 2- to 3-lb chicken)
- 4 kaiser rolls, split
- 2 cups deli coleslaw

1 In 2-quart saucepan, heat sauce ingredients to boiling over medium heat, stirring frequently. Reduce heat to medium-low; simmer uncovered 20 minutes, stirring occasionally. Remove and discard garlic.

2 Add shredded chicken to sauce; stir until evenly coated. Cook over low heat, stirring constantly, until chicken is hot.

3 Spoon about 1 cup chicken mixture onto each roll bottom; top with ½ cup coleslaw. Cover with bun tops.

1 Sandwich: Calories 560; Total Fat 23g (Saturated Fat 4.5g; Trans Fat 1g); Cholesterol 100mg; Sodium 1160mg; Total Carbohydrate 53g (Dietary Fiber 3g); Protein 36g **Exchanges:** 2 Starch, 1½ Other Carbohydrate, 4 Lean Meat, 2 Fat **Carbohydrate Choices:** 3½

CHAPTER 4

In the Pot

chicken and broth

Prep Time: 25 Minutes • **Start to Finish:** 1 Hour 20 Minutes • 4 servings (1 cup broth and about ½ cup chicken each)

1 whole or cut-up chicken (3 to 3½ lb)
1 teaspoon salt
½ teaspoon pepper
1 medium stalk celery with leaves, cut up
1 medium carrot, cut up
1 small onion, cut up
1 sprig fresh parsley
4½ cups cold water

1 In 4-quart Dutch oven or stockpot, place chicken. Add remaining ingredients; heat to boiling. Skim foam from broth; reduce heat. Cover; simmer about 45 minutes or until juice of chicken is clear when thickest pieces are cut to bone (at least 165°F).

2 Carefully remove chicken from broth (if using whole chicken, place wooden spoon into cavity and lift with fork or tongs). Cool chicken about 10 minutes or just until cool enough to handle. Strain broth through fine-mesh strainer; discard vegetables.

3 Remove skin and bones from chicken; discard. Cut chicken into ½-inch pieces. Skim fat from broth. Use broth and chicken immediately, or cover and refrigerate broth and chicken in separate containers up to 24 hours, or freeze up to 6 months.

Slow Cooker Directions: Decrease water to 3 cups. Increase salt to 1¼ teaspoons. Spray 5- to 6-quart slow cooker with cooking spray. In slow cooker, mix all ingredients. Cover; cook on Low heat setting 8 to 10 hours. Continue as directed in step 2.

1 Serving: Calories 180; Total Fat 7g (Saturated Fat 2g; Trans Fat 0g); Cholesterol 85mg; Sodium 490mg; Total Carbohydrate 2g (Dietary Fiber 0g); Protein 27g **Exchanges:** 4 Very Lean Meat, 1 Fat **Carbohydrate Choices:** 0

chicken noodle soup

Prep Time: 15 Minutes • **Start to Finish:** 40 Minutes • 6 servings (1 cup each)

1 carton (32 oz) chicken broth (4 cups)

1 cup water

4 medium carrots, sliced (2 cups)

4 medium stalks celery, sliced (2 cups)

1 medium onion, chopped (½ cup)

2½ to 3 cups cut-up cooked chicken

1 cup uncooked medium egg noodles (2 oz)

Chopped fresh parsley, if desired

1 In 4-quart Dutch oven or stockpot, stir together broth, water, carrots, celery and onion. Heat to boiling; reduce heat. Cover; simmer about 15 minutes or until carrots are tender.

2 Stir in chicken and noodles. Heat to boiling; reduce heat. Simmer uncovered 7 to 10 minutes or until noodles are tender. Sprinkle with parsley.

1 Serving: Calories 240; Total Fat 8g (Saturated Fat 2g; Trans Fat 0g); Cholesterol 90mg; Sodium 990mg; Total Carbohydrate 14g (Dietary Fiber 3g); Protein 29g **Exchanges:** ½ Starch, 1 Vegetable, 3½ Very Lean Meat, 1 Fat **Carbohydrate Choices:** 1

a new twist

For a variation with rice, substitute ½ cup uncooked regular long-grain white rice for the noodles. Stir in rice with the vegetables in step 1. Cover; simmer about 15 minutes or until rice is tender. Stir in chicken; heat until hot.

For a variation with more vegetables, add ½ cup each frozen sweet peas and corn with chicken and noodles in step 2. Continue as directed.

roasted chicken and broth

Prep Time: 20 Minutes • **Start to Finish:** 2 Hours 10 Minutes • **4 cups broth and 4 cups cooked chicken (1 cup broth and about ½ cup chicken each)**

CHICKEN AND VEGETABLES

- 1 cut-up whole chicken (3 to 3½ lb)
- 2 medium carrots
- 2 medium stalks celery
- 1 medium onion, quartered

BROTH

- 1 teaspoon salt
- ½ teaspoon pepper
- 1 medium stalk celery with leaves, cut up
- 1 medium carrot, cut up
- 1 small onion, cut up
- 1 sprig fresh parsley
- 5 cups cold water

1 Heat oven to 400°F. In ungreased 15x10x1-inch pan, arrange chicken and vegetables ingredients. Roast 1 hour to 1 hour 15 minutes or until chicken is medium to deep golden brown and pan juices are deep golden brown.

2 When cool enough to handle, remove chicken from carcass, reserving carcass, skin, pan juices and any browned bits from bottom of pan. Cut chicken into ½-inch pieces; cover and refrigerate. Discard, carrots, celery and onion from pan.

3 In 4- to 6-quart Dutch oven or stockpot, place chicken bones, skin, all pan juices and any browned bits. Add broth ingredients; heat to boiling. Skim foam from broth; reduce heat. Cover; simmer about 30 minutes to develop flavors.

4 Carefully remove bones and skin from broth. Strain broth through fine-mesh strainer; discard strainer contents. Skim fat from broth. Use broth and chicken immediately, or cover and refrigerate broth and chicken in separate containers up to 24 hours, or freeze up to 6 months.

1 Serving: Calories 220; Total Fat 9g (Saturated Fat 2.5g; Trans Fat 0g); Cholesterol 105mg; Sodium 700mg; Total Carbohydrate 0g (Dietary Fiber 0g); Protein 34g
Exchanges: 5 Very Lean Meat, 1 Fat **Carbohydrate Choices:** 0

swap it out

Use parsnips instead of carrots in the roasted mixture if you prefer.

root vegetable chicken soup

Prep Time: 25 Minutes • **Start to Finish:** 40 Minutes • 6 servings

2 tablespoons butter

3 medium carrots, thinly sliced (1 cup)

3 medium parsnips, peeled, thinly sliced (1 cup)

2 medium leeks, rinsed, cut in half lengthwise and sliced into ½-inch pieces (2 cups)

4 cups broth from Roasted Chicken and Broth (page 194)

⅓ cup uncooked orzo or rosamarina pasta (2 oz)

2 cups chopped cooked chicken from Roasted Chicken and Broth (page 194)

2 tablespoons chopped fresh or 2 teaspoons dried dill weed

1 In 4-quart Dutch oven or stockpot, melt butter over medium heat. Cook carrots, parsnips and leeks in butter 3 to 5 minutes, stirring occasionally, until carrots and parsnips are crisp-tender.

2 Stir in broth and pasta. Heat to boiling; reduce heat to low. Cover; simmer 10 to 12 minutes, stirring occasionally, until pasta is tender.

3 Stir in chicken and dill; cook until thoroughly heated.

1 Serving: Calories 230; Total Fat 8g (Saturated Fat 3.5g; Trans Fat 0g); Cholesterol 50mg; Sodium 480mg; Total Carbohydrate 23g (Dietary Fiber 4g); Protein 17g
Exchanges: ½ Starch, 1 Other Carbohydrate, ½ Vegetable, 2 Very Lean Meat, 1½ Fat
Carbohydrate Choices: 1½

swap it out

If dill isn't a flavor you enjoy, go ahead and use basil instead.

italian chicken noodle soup

Prep Time: 25 Minutes • **Start to Finish:** 35 Minutes • 6 servings (1½ cups each)

1 tablespoon olive or vegetable oil

½ lb boneless skinless chicken breasts, cut into ½-inch pieces

1 medium onion, chopped (½ cup)

1 carton (32 oz) chicken broth (4 cups)

2 cups water

3 medium carrots, sliced (1½ cups)

2 cups fresh broccoli florets

1½ cups uncooked egg noodles (3 oz)

1 teaspoon dried basil leaves

½ teaspoon garlic-pepper blend

¼ cup shredded Parmesan cheese (1 oz)

1 In 4-quart Dutch oven or stockpot, heat oil over medium heat. Cook chicken in oil 4 to 6 minutes, stirring occasionally, until no longer pink in center. Add onion. Cook 2 to 3 minutes, stirring occasionally, until onion is tender.

2 Stir in broth, water and carrots. Heat to boiling over medium heat. Cook 5 minutes. Stir in broccoli, noodles, basil and garlic-pepper blend. Heat to boiling; reduce heat. Simmer uncovered 8 to 10 minutes, stirring occasionally, until vegetables and noodles are tender.

3 Top individual servings with cheese.

1 Serving: Calories 170; Total Fat 6g (Saturated Fat 2g; Trans Fat 0g); Cholesterol 35mg; Sodium 710mg; Total Carbohydrate 13g (Dietary Fiber 2g); Protein 15g **Exchanges:** 1 Starch, 1½ Very Lean Meat, 1 Fat **Carbohydrate Choices:** 1

swap it out

You can substitute chicken thighs for part or all of the chicken breasts. And you can use frozen carrots and broccoli instead of fresh if you like.

chicken and pastina soup

Prep Time: 30 Minutes • **Start to Finish:** 45 Minutes • 10 servings (1½ cups each)

2 lb boneless skinless chicken breasts

2 cartons (32 oz each) chicken broth (8 cups)

1 tablespoon olive oil

1 medium onion (½ cup)

1 medium carrot (½ cup)

1 medium stalk celery, diced (½ cup)

1 cup crushed tomatoes with basil (from 28-oz can)

½ teaspoon coarse sea salt

¼ teaspoon pepper

1 dried bay leaf

1 cup uncooked acini di pepe pasta or other small round pasta (8 oz)

2 cups chopped lightly packed mustard greens, spinach or Swiss chard

⅓ cup shredded Parmesan cheese

Freshly ground pepper, if desired

1 Place chicken in 12-inch skillet. Add 1 carton of the broth. Heat to boiling; reduce heat. Cover; simmer 20 minutes or until juice of chicken is clear when center of thickest part is cut (at least 165°F).

2 Meanwhile, in 5-quart Dutch oven or stockpot, heat oil over medium heat. Cook onion, carrot and celery in oil 8 to 10 minutes, stirring occasionally, until tender.

3 Drain chicken, reserving broth; set chicken aside. Strain broth; add to vegetables. Stir in remaining carton of broth, the tomatoes, salt, pepper and bay leaf. Heat to boiling. Stir in pasta. Reduce heat. Cover; simmer 15 minutes.

4 Shred or cut chicken into bite-size pieces; add to soup. Stir in greens just until wilted. Remove bay leaf.

5 Top individual servings with cheese and a sprinkle of freshly ground pepper.

1 Serving: Calories 260; Total Fat 6g (Saturated Fat 2g; Trans Fat 0g); Cholesterol 60mg; Sodium 950mg; Total Carbohydrate 23g (Dietary Fiber 2g); Protein 28g **Exchanges:** 1 Starch, 1 Vegetable, 3 Very Lean Meat, 1 Fat **Carbohydrate Choices:** 1½

chicken-tortellini soup

Prep Time: 20 Minutes • **Start to Finish:** 1 Hour • 10 servings (1½ cups each)

6 cups water

½ cup dry vermouth
  or water

3 cans (10½ oz each)
  condensed chicken broth

1 can (10¾ oz) condensed
  cream of chicken soup

2 cups cubed
  cooked chicken

1 large onion, chopped
  (1 cup)

2 medium carrots, sliced
  (1 cup)

½ teaspoon dried
  basil leaves

½ teaspoon dried
  oregano leaves

2 cloves garlic,
  finely chopped

1 package (7 oz) dried
  cheese-filled tortellini

1 box (9 oz) frozen cut
  broccoli, thawed

¼ cup grated Parmesan
  cheese, if desired

1 In 5-quart Dutch oven or stockpot, stir together all ingredients except tortellini, broccoli and cheese. Heat to boiling. Stir in tortellini. Reduce heat; simmer uncovered 30 minutes, stirring occasionally.

2 Stir in broccoli; simmer 5 to 10 minutes longer or until broccoli is crisp-tender. Sprinkle individual servings with cheese.

1 Serving: Calories 170; Total Fat 4g (Saturated Fat 1.5g, Trans Fat 0g); Cholesterol 35mg; Sodium 570mg; Total Carbohydrate 17g (Dietary Fiber 1g); Protein 12g **Exchanges:** 1 Starch, ½ Vegetable, 1 Very Lean Meat, ½ Fat **Carbohydrate Choices:** 1

asian mushroom chicken soup

Prep Time: 30 Minutes • **Start to Finish:** 45 Minutes • **6 servings**

1½ cups water

1 package (1 oz) dried portabella or shiitake mushrooms

1 tablespoon canola oil

4 medium green onions, thinly sliced (¼ cup)

2 tablespoons finely chopped gingerroot

3 cloves garlic, finely chopped

1 jalapeño chile, seeded, finely chopped

1 cup fresh snow pea pods, cut diagonally in half

3 cups reduced-sodium chicken broth

1 can (8 oz) sliced bamboo shoots, drained

2 tablespoons reduced-sodium soy sauce

½ teaspoon Sriracha sauce

1 cup shredded cooked chicken breast

1 cup cooked brown rice

4 teaspoons lime juice

½ cup thinly sliced fresh basil leaves

1 In medium microwavable bowl, heat water uncovered on High 30 seconds or until hot. Add mushrooms; let stand 5 minutes or until tender. Drain and reserve liquid. Slice any mushrooms that are large; set aside.

2 In 4-quart Dutch oven or stockpot, heat oil over medium heat. Add 2 tablespoons of the onions, the gingerroot, garlic and chile. Cook about 3 minutes, stirring occasionally, until vegetables are tender. Add pea pods; cook 2 minutes, stirring occasionally.

3 Stir in broth, bamboo shoots, soy sauce, Sriracha sauce, chicken, rice, mushrooms and reserved mushroom liquid. Heat to boiling; reduce heat. Cover; simmer 10 minutes or until hot. Stir in lime juice.

4 Top individual servings evenly with basil and remaining 2 tablespoons onions.

1 Serving: Calories 150; Total Fat 4g (Saturated Fat 0.5g; Trans Fat 0g); Cholesterol 20mg; Sodium 490mg; Total Carbohydrate 16g (Dietary Fiber 3g); Protein 11g **Exchanges:** ½ Starch, 1½ Vegetable, 1 Very Lean Meat, ½ Fat **Carbohydrate Choices:** 1

thai chicken soup

Prep Time: 30 Minutes • **Start to Finish:** 30 Minutes • 6 servings (1 cup each)

1 teaspoon canola oil

1 small onion, cut into thin wedges (1 cup)

2 cups sliced fresh mushrooms (6 oz)

½ medium red bell pepper, cut into thin bite-size strips (1 cup)

2 cloves garlic, finely chopped

1 teaspoon red curry paste

1 carton (32 oz) reduced-sodium chicken broth (4 cups)

1½ cups shredded cooked chicken breast

1 teaspoon packed brown sugar

¼ teaspoon salt

1 tablespoon cornstarch

2 tablespoons cold water

1 can (14 oz) reduced-fat (lite) coconut milk (not cream of coconut)

4 cups fresh baby spinach leaves

2 tablespoons chopped fresh cilantro

Lime wedges, if desired

1 In 4-quart nonstick Dutch oven or stockpot, heat oil over medium heat. Add onion and mushrooms; cook 3 minutes, stirring frequently. Add bell pepper and garlic; cook 2 to 3 minutes longer, stirring frequently, until vegetables are tender. Remove from heat; stir in curry paste until melted.

2 Stir in broth, chicken, brown sugar and salt. Heat to boiling; reduce heat. Simmer uncovered 5 minutes, stirring frequently.

3 In small bowl, stir cornstarch and water until smooth. Add cornstarch mixture and coconut milk to soup mixture; heat to boiling. Cook over medium heat about 2 minutes, stirring frequently, until slightly thickened.

4 Stir in spinach and cilantro. Cook about 1 minute or just until mixture is hot and spinach is wilted. Serve soup with lime wedges.

1 Serving: Calories 150; Total Fat 7g (Saturated Fat 4g; Trans Fat 0g); Cholesterol 30mg; Sodium 550mg; Total Carbohydrate 8g (Dietary Fiber 1g); Protein 14g **Exchanges:** ½ Other Carbohydrate, 2 Lean Meat **Carbohydrate Choices:** ½

a new twist

For a spicier soup, add ½ to 1 teaspoon additional curry paste.

swap it out

If you don't have cornstarch, you can use 2 tablespoons all-purpose flour instead. Increase the amount of cold water to ¼ cup.

spicy chicken curry soup

Prep Time: 15 Minutes • **Start to Finish:** 15 Minutes • 4 servings (1½ cups each)

1 carton (32 oz) chicken broth (4 cups)

3 tablespoons packed brown sugar

2 tablespoons soy sauce

2 tablespoons rice vinegar

2 teaspoons curry powder

1 small red bell pepper, coarsely chopped (½ cup)

1 small jalapeño chile, seeded, finely chopped (1 tablespoon)

2 cups chopped deli rotisserie chicken (from 2- to 3-lb chicken)

2 tablespoons chopped fresh cilantro, if desired

1 In 3-quart saucepan, mix all ingredients except chicken and cilantro. Heat to boiling over medium-high heat; reduce heat to medium. Simmer uncovered 3 to 5 minutes, stirring occasionally, until bell pepper is crisp-tender.

2 Stir in chicken. Cook 1 to 2 minutes longer or until chicken is hot. Just before serving, stir in cilantro.

1 Serving: Calories 210; Total Fat 7g (Saturated Fat 2g; Trans Fat 0g); Cholesterol 60mg; Sodium 1770mg; Total Carbohydrate 14g (Dietary Fiber 0g); Protein 25g **Exchanges:** 1 Other Carbohydrate, 3 Lean Meat **Carbohydrate Choices:** 1

a new twist

If you enjoy spicy food, add an additional tablespoon of finely chopped jalapeño chile to the soup.

chicken tortilla soup

Prep Time: 15 Minutes • **Start to Finish:** 35 Minutes • **4 servings**

3 teaspoons vegetable oil

4 soft corn tortillas (5 to 6 inch), cut into 2x½-inch strips

1 medium onion, chopped (½ cup)

3½ cups chicken broth

1 can (10 oz) diced tomatoes with green chiles, undrained

1½ cups shredded cooked chicken

1 tablespoon lime juice

1 tablespoon chopped fresh cilantro or parsley

1 In 2-quart nonstick saucepan, heat 2 teaspoons of the oil over medium-high heat. Add tortilla strips; cook 30 to 60 seconds, stirring constantly, until crisp and light golden brown. Drain on paper towels.

2 In same saucepan, heat remaining 1 teaspoon oil over medium-high heat. Cook onion in oil, stirring occasionally, until tender. Stir in broth and tomatoes. Heat to boiling; reduce heat. Simmer uncovered 20 minutes. Stir in chicken; heat until hot.

3 Stir in lime juice. Sprinkle tortilla strips on top of soup, or spoon soup over tortilla strips. Sprinkle with cilantro.

1 Serving: Calories 230; Total Fat 8g (Saturated Fat 1.5g; Trans Fat 0g); Cholesterol 45mg; Sodium 1100mg; Total Carbohydrate 17g (Dietary Fiber 3g); Protein 22g **Exchanges:** 1 Starch, 2½ Very Lean Meat, 1 Fat **Carbohydrate Choices:** 1

cheesy chicken enchilada soup

Prep Time: 20 Minutes • **Start to Finish:** 20 Minutes • 6 servings (1 cup each)

2   cans (10¾ oz each) condensed 98% fat-free cream of chicken soup with 30% less sodium

1   can (10 oz) enchilada sauce

2   cups milk

1   cup shredded reduced-fat Cheddar cheese (4 oz)

1   package (9 oz) frozen cooked southwestern-seasoned chicken breast strips, thawed, chopped (2 cups)

¾   cup crushed tortilla chips

1 In 3-quart saucepan, mix all ingredients except tortilla chips. Cook over medium heat, stirring occasionally, until thoroughly heated and cheese is melted.

2 Top individual servings with tortilla chips.

1 Serving: Calories 260; Total Fat 11g (Saturated Fat 3g; Trans Fat 0.5g); Cholesterol 45mg; Sodium 1100mg; Total Carbohydrate 22g (Dietary Fiber 0g); Protein 19g **Exchanges:** 1 Starch, ½ Low-Fat Milk, 1½ Very Lean Meat, 1½ Fat **Carbohydrate Choices:** 1½

creole chicken soup

Prep Time: 35 Minutes • **Start to Finish:** 55 Minutes • 8 servings (1½ cups each)

2 tablespoons butter

2 medium onions, coarsely chopped (1 cup)

2 medium stalks celery, coarsely chopped (1 cup)

1 medium green bell pepper, coarsely chopped (1 cup)

2 teaspoons finely chopped garlic

2½ lb boneless skinless chicken breasts or thighs, cut into 1-inch pieces

¼ cup all-purpose flour

1 carton (32 oz) reduced-sodium chicken broth (4 cups)

2 cans (14.5 oz each) diced tomatoes, undrained

2 cups water

1 cup uncooked regular long-grain rice

1 teaspoon salt

¼ teaspoon ground red pepper (cayenne)

2 dried bay leaves

1 In 5-quart Dutch oven or stockpot, melt butter over medium-high heat. Add onions, celery, bell pepper, garlic and chicken. Cook 7 to 9 minutes, stirring frequently, until onion is softened.

2 Stir in flour. Cook 5 to 6 minutes, stirring constantly, until flour is light brown.

3 Stir in remaining ingredients. Heat to boiling; reduce heat to medium-low. Cover; cook 15 to 20 minutes, stirring occasionally, until rice is tender and chicken is no longer pink in center. Remove bay leaves before serving.

1 Serving: Calories 340; Total Fat 8g (Saturated Fat 3g; Trans Fat 0g); Cholesterol 95mg; Sodium 810mg; Total Carbohydrate 31g (Dietary Fiber 2g); Protein 36g **Exchanges:** 1½ Starch, 1 Vegetable, 4½ Very Lean Meat, 1 Fat **Carbohydrate Choices:** 2

chili chicken soup with cilantro dumplings

Prep Time: 20 Minutes • **Start to Finish:** 45 Minutes • 5 servings

SOUP

- 1 tablespoon vegetable oil
- 1¼ lb boneless skinless chicken breasts, cut into 1-inch cubes
- 1 medium onion, chopped (½ cup)
- 3 teaspoons chili powder
- ½ to 1 teaspoon salt
- 5 cups chicken broth

DUMPLINGS

- 2 cups Original Bisquick™ mix
- ⅔ cup milk
- ½ cup chopped fresh cilantro
- ½ teaspoon ground cumin
- 1 jalapeño chile, seeded, chopped, if desired

1 In 3-quart saucepan, heat oil over medium heat. Add chicken, onion, chili powder and salt; cook, stirring frequently, until chicken is browned. Stir in broth. Heat to boiling; reduce heat to medium. Simmer uncovered 5 minutes.

2 Meanwhile, in medium bowl, stir Bisquick mix and milk until soft dough forms. Fold in cilantro, cumin and chile.

3 Drop dough by 10 spoonfuls onto simmering soup. Cook uncovered 10 minutes. Cover; cook 10 minutes longer.

1 Serving: Calories 400; Total Fat 13g (Saturated Fat 3.5g; Trans Fat 2g); Cholesterol 75mg; Sodium 1770mg; Total Carbohydrate 36g (Dietary Fiber 2g); Protein 33g
Exchanges: 2½ Starch, 3½ Lean Meat **Carbohydrate Choices:** 2½

hearty chicken stew with dumplings

Prep Time: 10 Minutes • **Start to Finish:** 30 Minutes • 3 servings

2 cups frozen broccoli, carrots and cauliflower (from 1-lb bag)

1 cup cut-up cooked chicken breast

¾ cup water

1 tablespoon ketchup

½ teaspoon Italian seasoning

¼ teaspoon garlic salt

⅛ teaspoon pepper

1 can (14.5 oz) no-salt-added stewed tomatoes, undrained

1 cup Bisquick™ Heart Smart mix

⅓ cup fat-free (skim) milk

½ teaspoon parsley flakes

1 In 2-quart saucepan, stir together frozen vegetables, chicken, water, ketchup, Italian seasoning, ⅛ teaspoon of the garlic salt, the pepper and tomatoes. Heat to boiling, stirring occasionally.

2 In small bowl, stir Bisquick mix, milk, parsley flakes and remaining ⅛ teaspoon garlic salt until soft dough forms.

3 Drop dough by 6 spoonfuls onto boiling stew; reduce heat. Simmer uncovered 10 minutes. Cover; simmer 10 minutes longer.

1 Serving: Calories 300; Total Fat 4.5g (Saturated Fat 0.5g; Trans Fat 0g); Cholesterol 40mg; Sodium 530mg; Total Carbohydrate 43g (Dietary Fiber 3g); Protein 22g
Exchanges: 1½ Starch, 1 Other Carbohydrate, 1 Vegetable, 2 Very Lean Meat, ½ Fat
Carbohydrate Choices: 3

swap it out

Dried basil leaves make a good stand-in for the Italian seasoning.

chicken-vegetable soup with dumplings

Prep Time: 10 Minutes • **Start to Finish:** 35 Minutes • 6 servings (1 cup each)

2 cups cut-up cooked chicken

1 carton (32 oz) chicken broth (4 cups)

1 tablespoon chopped fresh parsley

1 tablespoon chopped fresh thyme leaves

2 cloves garlic, finely chopped

2⅔ cups frozen mixed vegetables (from 12-oz bag), thawed, drained

1 cup Original Bisquick™ mix

⅓ cup milk

1 In 3-quart saucepan, stir together chicken, broth, parsley, thyme, garlic and vegetables. Heat to boiling, stirring occasionally.

2 In small bowl, stir Bisquick mix and milk with fork until soft dough forms.

3 Drop dough by 18 teaspoonfuls onto boiling soup. (If dumplings sink into soup, carefully bring them to top using slotted spoon.) Reduce heat to medium-low. Cook uncovered 10 minutes. Cover; cook 15 minutes longer.

1 Serving: Calories 210; Total Fat 7g (Saturated Fat 2g; Trans Fat 0.5g); Cholesterol 40mg; Sodium 1030mg; Total Carbohydrate 17g (Dietary Fiber 2g); Protein 20g **Exchanges:** 1 Starch, 2½ Lean Meat **Carbohydrate Choices:** 1

summer chicken soup with biscuit dumplings

Prep Time: 35 Minutes • **Start to Finish:** 50 Minutes • 6 servings (1½ cups each)

SOUP

- 1 tablespoon vegetable oil
- 1 medium onion, chopped (½ cup)
- 2 cloves garlic, finely chopped
- 1 carton (32 oz) chicken broth (4 cups)
- 12 ready-to-eat baby-cut carrots, cut in half lengthwise
- 4 cups shredded cooked chicken
- 1 medium zucchini, cut into cubes
- 1 medium yellow summer squash, cut into cubes
- 1 box (9 oz) frozen baby sweet peas, thawed
- ½ teaspoon salt
- ¼ teaspoon pepper
- ¼ cup chopped fresh dill weed

DUMPLINGS

- 1 can (10.2 oz) large refrigerated flaky biscuits (5 biscuits)
- ¼ cup chopped fresh parsley

1 In 4-quart Dutch oven or stockpot, heat oil over medium-high heat. Cook onion and garlic in oil about 2 minutes, stirring frequently, until onion is tender. Add broth; heat to boiling.

2 Add carrots; reduce heat to medium. Cook about 5 minutes or until carrots are tender. Add remaining soup ingredients. Heat to boiling over high heat; reduce heat to medium-high. Cover; cook 2 to 3 minutes or until vegetables are crisp-tender.

3 Cut each biscuit into quarters. Dip one side of each biscuit piece in parsley. Drop biscuits parsley side up onto hot soup. Reduce heat to medium. Cover; cook 10 to 15 minutes or until dumplings are no longer doughy in center.

1 Serving: Calories 400; Total Fat 14g (Saturated Fat 3g; Trans Fat 3g); Cholesterol 75mg; Sodium 1340mg; Total Carbohydrate 32g (Dietary Fiber 3g); Protein 36g **Exchanges:** 2 Starch, 1 Vegetable, 4 Lean Meat **Carbohydrate Choices:** 2

chicken chili with cornbread dumplings

Prep Time: 15 Minutes • **Start to Finish:** 30 Minutes • 6 servings

CHILI

- 3 cups cubed cooked chicken
- 1½ cups water
- 1 can (10¾ oz) condensed cream of chicken soup
- 1 can (15 oz) navy beans, drained, rinsed
- 1 can (11 oz) whole kernel corn with red and green peppers, undrained
- 1 can (4.5 oz) chopped green chiles
- 1 teaspoon ground cumin

DUMPLINGS

- 1⅓ cups Original Bisquick™ mix
- ⅔ cup yellow cornmeal
- ⅔ cup milk
- 1 teaspoon chili powder

1 In 5-quart nonstick Dutch oven or stockpot, heat chili ingredients over medium-high heat, stirring occasionally, until bubbly.

2 Meanwhile, in medium bowl, stir dumpling ingredients until soft dough forms.

3 Drop dough by 6 rounded spoonfuls onto simmering chili. Reduce heat to medium-low. Cover; cook 13 to 15 minutes or until dumplings are dry.

1 Serving: Calories 490; Total Fat 13g (Saturated Fat 4g; Trans Fat 1g); Cholesterol 65mg; Sodium 1160mg; Total Carbohydrate 61g (Dietary Fiber 7g); Protein 30g **Exchanges:** 3½ Starch, ½ Other Carbohydrate, 2½ Medium-Fat Meat **Carbohydrate Choices:** 4

green chile, chicken and bean chili

Prep Time: 30 Minutes • **Start to Finish:** 55 Minutes • 5 servings (1½ cups each)

1 tablespoon olive or vegetable oil

1 large onion, coarsely chopped (1 cup)

2 teaspoons finely chopped garlic

1 tablespoon ground cumin

1 teaspoon salt

⅛ teaspoon ground red pepper (cayenne)

2 lb boneless skinless chicken thighs, cut into ½-inch pieces

2 cans (15 to 16 oz each) great northern beans, drained, rinsed

2 cans (4.5 oz each) chopped green chiles, undrained

2 cups chicken broth

Chopped fresh cilantro, if desired

1 In 4½- to 5-quart Dutch oven or stockpot, heat oil over medium-high heat. Add onions and garlic; cook 4 to 5 minutes, stirring frequently, until onions are softened.

2 Stir in cumin, salt, red pepper and chicken. Cook 6 to 7 minutes, stirring occasionally, until chicken is lightly browned.

3 Stir in beans, chiles and broth. Heat to boiling. Reduce heat to medium-low. Cover; cook 20 to 25 minutes, stirring occasionally, until chicken is no longer pink in center. Sprinkle with cilantro.

1 Serving: Calories 560; Total Fat 19g (Saturated Fat 5g; Trans Fat 0g); Cholesterol 115mg; Sodium 1750mg; Total Carbohydrate 42g (Dietary Fiber 11g); Protein 55g **Exchanges:** 3 Starch, 6 Lean Meat **Carbohydrate Choices:** 3

spicy chicken chili

Prep Time: 20 Minutes • **Start to Finish:** 20 Minutes • 4 servings (1¼ cups each)

1 lb boneless skinless chicken breasts, cut into ¾-inch pieces

1 can (14.5 oz) salsa-style chunky tomatoes, undrained

1 can (15 oz) spicy chili beans in sauce, undrained

½ cup shredded Cheddar cheese (2 oz)

1 Spray 3-quart saucepan with cooking spray; heat over medium-high heat. Add chicken; cook 3 to 5 minutes, stirring frequently, until light brown.

2 Stir in tomatoes and beans; reduce heat to medium-low. Cook uncovered 8 to 10 minutes, stirring frequently, until chicken is no longer pink in center. Top individual servings with cheese.

1 Serving: Calories 310; Total Fat 9g (Saturated Fat 4g; Trans Fat 0g); Cholesterol 85mg; Sodium 1270mg; Total Carbohydrate 23g (Dietary Fiber 3g); Protein 34g **Exchanges:** ½ Starch, ½ Other Carbohydrate, 1 Vegetable, 4 Very Lean Meat, ½ High-Fat Meat, ½ Fat **Carbohydrate Choices:** 1½

buffalo chicken chili

Prep Time: 35 Minutes • **Start to Finish:** 35 Minutes • 6 servings (1½ cups each)

1 tablespoon vegetable oil

1 large onion, chopped (1 cup)

1 medium red or yellow bell pepper, chopped (1 cup)

2 cups cubed deli rotisserie chicken (from 2- to 3-lb chicken)

1 cup chicken broth

1 tablespoon chili powder

5 or 6 drops red pepper sauce

2 cans (15 oz each) pinto beans, drained, rinsed

1 can (28 oz) crushed tomatoes, undrained

1 can (14.5 oz) diced tomatoes, undrained

½ cup sliced celery

½ cup crumbled blue cheese (2 oz)

1 In 3-quart saucepan, heat oil over medium-high heat. Cook onion and bell pepper in oil about 5 minutes, stirring occasionally, until crisp-tender.

2 Stir in all remaining ingredients except celery and cheese. Heat to boiling; reduce heat to medium-low. Simmer uncovered 10 to 15 minutes, stirring occasionally. Top individual servings with celery and cheese.

1 Serving: Calories 380; Total Fat 10g (Saturated Fat 3.5g; Trans Fat 0g); Cholesterol 50mg; Sodium 1060mg; Total Carbohydrate 43g (Dietary Fiber 13g); Protein 28g **Exchanges:** 2½ Starch, 1 Vegetable, 2½ Lean Meat, ½ Fat **Carbohydrate Choices:** 3

a new twist

To make it "Cincinnati-style," serve the chili over hot cooked spaghetti.

white chicken and corn chili

Prep Time: 20 Minutes • **Start to Finish:** 45 Minutes • 6 servings (1⅓ cups each)

1 tablespoon vegetable oil

1 large onion, chopped (1 cup)

2 cloves garlic, finely chopped

3 cups chicken broth (from 32-oz carton)

1 can (15.5 oz) great northern beans, drained

1 can (15.5 oz) butter beans, drained

1 can (11 oz) white shoepeg or whole kernel sweet corn, drained

2 tablespoons chopped fresh cilantro

2 tablespoons lime juice

1 teaspoon ground cumin

½ teaspoon dried oregano leaves

¼ teaspoon red pepper sauce

¼ teaspoon salt

2 cups chopped cooked chicken breast

1 In 4-quart Dutch oven or stockpot, heat oil over medium heat. Cook onion and garlic in oil 4 to 6 minutes, stirring occasionally, until onion is tender.

2 Stir in all remaining ingredients except chicken. Heat to boiling; reduce heat. Simmer uncovered 20 minutes. Stir in chicken; simmer about 5 minutes longer or until hot.

1 Serving: Calories 360; Total Fat 6g (Saturated Fat 1.5g; Trans Fat 0g); Cholesterol 40mg; Sodium 920mg; Total Carbohydrate 46g (Dietary Fiber 11g); Protein 31g **Exchanges:** 2 Starch, 3 Vegetable, 2 Lean Meat **Carbohydrate Choices:** 3

chicken mole chili

Prep Time: 15 Minutes   •   **Start to Finish:** 30 Minutes   •   5 servings (1½ cups each)

1 tablespoon vegetable oil

1 large onion, chopped (1 cup)

2 cups chicken broth

1 jar (16 oz) chunky-style salsa

2 cans (15 oz each) pinto beans, drained, rinsed

1 can (4.5 oz) chopped green chiles

1 package (1.25 oz) chili seasoning mix

1 oz bittersweet baking chocolate, grated

⅛ teaspoon ground cinnamon

2 cups shredded cooked chicken

Sliced green onions, if desired

Tortilla chips, if desired

1 In 4-quart Dutch oven or stockpot, heat oil over medium-high heat. Cook onion in oil about 2 minutes, stirring frequently, or until tender.

2 Stir in broth, salsa, beans, chiles, chili seasoning mix, chocolate and cinnamon. Heat to boiling, stirring occasionally; reduce heat to low. Cover; simmer 10 to 15 minutes.

3 Stir in chicken; cook 2 to 3 minutes longer or until chicken is hot. Top individual servings with green onions. Serve with tortilla chips.

1 Serving: Calories 390; Total Fat 9g (Saturated Fat 3g; Trans Fat 0g); Cholesterol 45mg; Sodium 1600mg; Total Carbohydrate 47g (Dietary Fiber 13g); Protein 30g **Exchanges:** 3 Starch, 1 Vegetable, 2½ Lean Meat **Carbohydrate Choices:** 3

a new twist

To make taco or enchilada filling, reduce broth to 1 cup. Spoon chicken mixture into warmed taco shells or flour tortillas. Top with shredded Cheddar or pepper Jack cheese and your favorite taco toppings.

chicken pozole

Prep Time: 35 Minutes • **Start to Finish:** 1 Hour 15 Minutes • 12 servings

6 dried guajillo chiles, stems and seeds removed

6 dried ancho chiles, stems and seeds removed

1½ cups water

2 tablespoons olive oil

1 small onion, coarsely chopped (¼ cup)

1 clove garlic

2 cartons (32 oz each) chicken broth (8 cups)

1 teaspoon kosher (coarse) salt

1 teaspoon dried oregano leaves

1 teaspoon chicken bouillon granules

½ teaspoon dried thyme leaves

2 dried bay leaves

1 sprig fresh parsley

2 cups shredded cooked chicken

2 cans (28 oz each) hominy, drained

1 In medium bowl, soak chiles in water about 20 minutes. (Do not drain.)

2 In 6-quart Dutch oven or stockpot, heat oil over medium heat. Cook onion and garlic in oil 1 to 2 minutes, stirring constantly, until onion is crisp-tender. Place in blender; add chiles in water. Cover; blend on high speed about 1 minute or until smooth.

3 Place strainer over Dutch oven; pour mixture from blender into strainer. Discard solids. Cook uncovered over medium heat 5 to 10 minutes, stirring occasionally, until flavors are blended.

4 Add remaining ingredients. Heat to boiling; reduce heat. Cover; simmer about 20 minutes, stirring occasionally, until flavors are blended. Remove bay leaves and parsley before serving.

1 Serving: Calories 210; Total Fat 6g (Saturated Fat 1g; Trans Fat 0g); Cholesterol 20mg; Sodium 1140mg; Total Carbohydrate 26g (Dietary Fiber 5g); Protein 12g **Exchanges:** 1½ Starch, 1 Lean Meat, ½ Fat **Carbohydrate Choices:** 2

black bean, chicken and rice stew

Prep Time: 30 Minutes • **Start to Finish:** 30 Minutes • 4 servings (1½ cups each)

2 teaspoons oil

1 cup uncooked regular long-grain white rice

1½ teaspoons ground cumin

1 teaspoon chili powder

2 cups cubed cooked chicken

2 cups frozen bell pepper and onion stir-fry (from 1-lb bag), thawed, coarsely chopped

1 can (15 oz) black beans, drained, rinsed

1¾ cups chicken broth

2 tablespoons water

½ cup shredded Cheddar cheese (2 oz)

1 In 3-quart saucepan, heat oil over medium-high heat. Add rice, cumin and chili powder; cook and stir 1 minute.

2 Stir in all remaining ingredients except cheese. Heat to boiling; reduce heat. Cover; simmer 15 to 18 minutes, stirring occasionally, until liquid is absorbed and rice is tender.

3 Remove from heat. Uncover; fluff mixture with fork. Sprinkle with cheese. Cover; let stand 1 to 2 minutes or until cheese is melted.

1 Serving: Calories 530; Total Fat 13g (Saturated Fat 5g, Trans Fat 0g); Cholesterol 75mg; Sodium 540mg; Total Carbohydrate 68g (Dietary Fiber 10g); Protein 35g
Exchanges: 4 Starch, ½ Other Carbohydrate, 3 Very Lean Meat, 2 Fat **Carbohydrate Choices:** 4½

swap it out

In place of the frozen stir-fry mixture, you can use 1¾ cups fresh red, yellow and green bell pepper strips plus ¼ cup chopped onion.

cheesy chicken-vegetable chowder

Prep Time: 20 Minutes • **Start to Finish:** 30 Minutes • 4 servings (1⅓ cups each)

1 tablespoon butter

1 medium onion, chopped (½ cup)

2 cups frozen mixed vegetables (from 12-oz bag)

2 cups frozen southern-style diced hash brown potatoes (from 32-oz bag)

2 cups cubed cooked chicken

1¾ cups chicken broth

6 oz Mexican prepared cheese product with jalapeño peppers (from 16-oz loaf), cut into cubes

1 In 3-quart saucepan, melt butter over medium heat. Cook onion in butter 2 to 3 minutes, stirring frequently, until crisp-tender.

2 Stir in vegetables, potatoes, chicken and broth. Heat to boiling; reduce heat. Cover; simmer 8 to 10 minutes or until vegetables and potatoes are tender.

3 Stir in cheese; cook over medium-low heat, stirring occasionally, until cheese is melted and smooth and soup is thoroughly heated.

1 Serving: Calories 450; Total Fat 17g (Saturated Fat 9g, Trans Fat 0.5g); Cholesterol 105mg; Sodium 1120mg; Total Carbohydrate 42g (Dietary Fiber 5g); Protein 31g **Exchanges:** 1 Starch, 1½ Other Carbohydrate, 1 Vegetable, 2½ Very Lean Meat, 1½ High-Fat Meat, ½ Fat **Carbohydrate Choices:** 3

swap it out

Use regular prepared cheese product instead of the Mexican-flavored cheese if you prefer less spice.

chicken taco stew in bread bowls

Prep Time: 35 Minutes • **Start to Finish:** 35 Minutes • 3 servings

1 can (11 oz) refrigerated crusty French loaf

1 package (6 oz) refrigerated cooked Southwest-flavor chicken breast strips, coarsely chopped

1 can (15 oz) dark-red kidney beans, drained, rinsed

1 can (10 oz) diced tomatoes with green chiles, undrained

1 cup frozen corn (from 12-oz bag)

1 cup chicken broth

1 tablespoon cornstarch

½ cup shredded Cheddar cheese (2 oz)

1 Heat oven to 350°F. Spray cookie sheet with cooking spray. Cut dough into 3 equal pieces. Shape each into a ball, placing seam at bottom so dough is smooth on top. Place dough balls seam side down on cookie sheet.

2 Bake 18 to 22 minutes or until golden brown. Cool 5 minutes.

3 Meanwhile, in 2-quart saucepan, mix all remaining ingredients except cheese. Cook over medium heat, stirring occasionally, until mixture boils and thickens.

4 Cut top off each bread loaf. Lightly press center of bread down to form bowls. Place each bread bowl in individual shallow soup plate. Spoon about 1 cup stew into each bread bowl. Sprinkle with cheese. Place top of each bread bowl next to filled bowl.

1 Serving: Calories 620; Total Fat 12g (Saturated Fat 6g; Trans Fat 0g); Cholesterol 45mg; Sodium 1400mg; Total Carbohydrate 90g (Dietary Fiber 9g); Protein 36g **Exchanges:** 4 Starch, 1½ Other Carbohydrate, 2 Vegetable, 3 Lean Meat **Carbohydrate Choices:** 6

french peasant chicken stew

Prep Time: 10 Minutes • **Start to Finish:** 35 Minutes • 6 servings (1⅓ cups each)

2 cups ready-to-eat baby-cut carrots

1 cup sliced fresh mushrooms (3 oz)

4 small red potatoes, cut into quarters

1 jar (12 oz) chicken gravy

1¾ cups reduced-sodium chicken broth

1 teaspoon dried thyme leaves

½ cup frozen baby sweet peas (from 12-oz bag)

1 deli rotisserie chicken (2 to 3 lb), cut into serving pieces

1 In 4-quart Dutch oven or stockpot, stir together carrots, mushrooms, potatoes, gravy, broth and thyme. Heat to boiling over medium-high heat; reduce heat to medium-low. Cover; simmer about 20 minutes or until vegetables are tender.

2 Stir in peas and chicken. Cover; simmer about 5 minutes longer or until peas are tender and chicken is hot.

1 Serving: Calories 290; Total Fat 10g (Saturated Fat 2.5g; Trans Fat 0g); Cholesterol 75mg; Sodium 920mg; Total Carbohydrate 22g (Dietary Fiber 4g); Protein 28g **Exchanges:** 1½ Starch, 1 Vegetable, 3 Lean Meat **Carbohydrate Choices:** 1½

a new twist

To make an elegant version of the recipe, add 2 tablespoons white wine with the broth mixture.

CHAPTER 5

From the Slow Cooker

rotisserie spiced chicken

Prep Time: 10 Minutes • **Start to Finish:** 4 Hours 10 Minutes • 4 servings

SPICE RUB

- 2 teaspoons paprika
- 1 teaspoon garlic salt
- 1 teaspoon onion powder
- 1 teaspoon sugar
- 1 teaspoon chili powder
- ½ teaspoon dried thyme leaves, crushed
- ½ teaspoon dried marjoram leaves, crushed
- ½ teaspoon pepper

CHICKEN

- 1 whole chicken (3½ to 4½ lb)

1 Spray 5- to 6-quart oval slow cooker with cooking spray. In small bowl, mix spice rub ingredients until well blended.

2 Rub spice mixture on all sides of chicken. Do not tie legs. Place chicken in slow cooker, making sure it fits loosely (leave at least 1 inch of space around chicken).

3 Cover; cook on Low heat setting 4 to 5 hours or until instant-read meat thermometer inserted in thickest part of inside thigh muscle and not touching bone reads at least 165°F and legs move easily when lifted or twisted. Do not remove slow cooker cover before 4 hours.

1 Serving: Calories 270; Total Fat 11g (Saturated Fat 3g; Trans Fat 0g); Cholesterol 125mg; Sodium 370mg; Total Carbohydrate 3g (Dietary Fiber 1g); Protein 40g **Exchanges:** 5½ Very Lean Meat, 1½ Fat **Carbohydrate Choices:** 0

a new twist

For a smoky flavor, use 1 teaspoon smoked paprika and 1 teaspoon regular paprika.

chicken and barley risotto with edamame

Prep Time: 20 Minutes • **Start to Finish:** 4 Hours 45 Minutes • 9 servings (1 cup each)

1¼ lb boneless skinless chicken breasts, cut into ¾-inch cubes

1½ cups chopped onions (3 medium)

1¼ cups uncooked pearl barley

½ cup shredded carrot

2 cloves garlic, finely chopped

½ teaspoon salt

½ teaspoon dried thyme leaves

1 carton (32 oz) chicken broth (4 cups)

1 cup frozen shelled edamame (green) soybeans, thawed

½ cup shredded Parmesan cheese (2 oz)

1 Spray 4- to 5-quart slow cooker with cooking spray. In slow cooker, mix chicken, onions, barley, carrot, garlic, salt, thyme and 3 cups of the broth.

2 Cover; cook on Low heat setting 4 to 5 hours.

3 In 2-cup microwavable measuring cup, microwave remaining 1 cup broth uncovered on High 2 to 3 minutes or until boiling. Stir thawed edamame and boiling broth into barley mixture in slow cooker. Increase heat setting to High. Cover; cook 25 to 30 minutes or until edamame is tender. Stir in cheese.

1 Serving: Calories 250; Total Fat 6g (Saturated Fat 2g; Trans Fat 0g); Cholesterol 45mg; Sodium 690mg; Total Carbohydrate 27g (Dietary Fiber 6g); Protein 23g **Exchanges:** 1½ Starch, 1 Vegetable, 2 Lean Meat **Carbohydrate Choices:** 2

a new twist

For a vegetarian version of this deliciously wholesome recipe, omit the chicken and use vegetable broth instead of chicken broth.

chicken parmesan with penne pasta

Prep Time: 15 Minutes • **Start to Finish:** 5 Hours 25 Minutes • 4 servings

1 egg

⅓ cup unseasoned dry bread crumbs

⅓ cup shredded Parmesan cheese

½ teaspoon Italian seasoning

¼ teaspoon salt

¼ teaspoon pepper

4 boneless skinless chicken breasts (about 1¼ lb)

1 jar (26 oz) tomato pasta sauce

½ cup shredded Italian cheese blend (2 oz)

2⅔ cups uncooked penne pasta (8 oz)

1 Spray 3½- to 4-quart slow cooker with cooking spray. In small shallow bowl, beat egg until foamy. In separate shallow bowl, mix bread crumbs, Parmesan cheese, Italian seasoning, salt and pepper. Dip chicken into egg, then coat evenly with bread crumb mixture; place in slow cooker. Spread pasta sauce evenly over chicken.

2 Cover; cook on Low heat setting 5 to 6 hours.

3 Sprinkle Italian cheese blend over top. Cover; cook 10 minutes longer.

4 Meanwhile, cook and drain pasta as directed on package. Serve chicken and sauce over pasta.

1 Serving: Calories 720; Total Fat 22g (Saturated Fat 7g; Trans Fat 0g); Cholesterol 200mg; Sodium 1730mg; Total Carbohydrate 79g (Dietary Fiber 5g); Protein 51g **Exchanges:** 3 Starch, 2 Other Carbohydrate, 6 Lean Meat, ½ Fat **Carbohydrate Choices:** 5

swap it out

For variety, experiment using different flavors of pasta sauces and any of your favorite pasta shapes.

chicken cacciatore with linguine

Prep Time: 25 Minutes • **Start to Finish:** 8 Hours 25 Minutes • 6 servings

2½ lb boneless skinless chicken thighs

1 jar (4.5 oz) sliced mushrooms, drained

2 cans (6 oz each) Italian-style tomato paste

1¾ cups chicken broth

½ cup white wine, if desired

1½ teaspoons dried basil leaves

½ teaspoon salt

1 dried bay leaf

1 tablespoon cornstarch

¼ teaspoon dried thyme leaves

12 oz uncooked linguine

Shredded Parmesan cheese, if desired

1 Spray 3½- to 4-quart slow cooker with cooking spray. Place chicken in slow cooker. Add mushrooms, tomato paste, broth, wine, basil, salt and bay leaf; gently stir to mix.

2 Cover; cook on Low heat setting 8 to 10 hours.

3 Remove chicken from slow cooker; cover to keep warm. Remove bay leaf. Increase heat setting to High. In small bowl, mix ¼ cup sauce from slow cooker and the cornstarch until smooth; stir into remaining sauce in slow cooker. Add thyme. Cover; cook 10 minutes, stirring frequently.

4 Meanwhile, cook and drain linguine as directed on package. Serve chicken and sauce over linguine. Sprinkle with cheese.

1 Serving: Calories 620; Total Fat 17g (Saturated Fat 5g; Trans Fat 0g); Cholesterol 120mg; Sodium 1110mg; Total Carbohydrate 63g (Dietary Fiber 6g); Protein 53g **Exchanges:** 2 Starch, 2 Other Carbohydrate, 1 Vegetable, 6 Lean Meat **Carbohydrate Choices:** 4

swap it out

One 26-ounce jar of tomato pasta sauce can be substituted for the tomato paste, chicken broth and white wine.

spicy chicken nachos

Prep Time: 15 Minutes • **Start to Finish:** 3 Hours • 24 servings (¼ cup chicken mixture and 7 chips each)

1 loaf (16 oz) Mexican prepared cheese product with jalapeño peppers, cut into cubes

¾ cup chunky-style salsa

1 can (15 oz) black beans, drained, rinsed

1 package (9 oz) frozen cooked chicken breast strips, thawed, cut into cubes

1 container (8 oz) sour cream

1 medium red bell pepper, chopped (1 cup)

3 medium green onions, sliced (3 tablespoons)

Large tortilla chips

1 Spray 3½- to 4-quart slow cooker with cooking spray. In slow cooker, stir together cheese, salsa, beans and chicken.

2 Cover; cook on Low heat setting 2 hours, stirring after 1 hour.

3 Increase heat setting to High. Stir in sour cream, bell pepper and onions. Cover; cook about 45 minutes or until mixture is hot.

4 Serve with tortilla chips. Chicken mixture can be kept warm on Low heat setting up to 2 hours; stir occasionally.

1 Serving: Calories 200; Total Fat 11g (Saturated Fat 4.5g; Trans Fat 0g); Cholesterol 25mg; Sodium 400mg; Total Carbohydrate 17g (Dietary Fiber 2g); Protein 9g **Exchanges:** 1 Starch, 1 High-Fat Meat, ½ Fat **Carbohydrate Choices:** 1

chile-chicken tacos

Prep Time: 15 Minutes • **Start to Finish:** 6 Hours 30 Minutes • 6 servings (2 tacos each)

1¼ lb boneless skinless chicken thighs

1 package (1 oz) taco seasoning mix

1 tablespoon packed brown sugar

1 can (4.5 oz) chopped green chiles

1 cup frozen corn (from 12-oz bag), thawed

1 can (10 oz) enchilada sauce

4 medium green onions, sliced (¼ cup)

1 box (4.6 oz) taco shells (12 shells), heated as directed on box

3 cups shredded lettuce

1 medium tomato, chopped (¾ cup)

1 Spray 3½- to 4-quart slow cooker with cooking spray. Place chicken in slow cooker. Sprinkle with taco seasoning mix and brown sugar; toss to coat. Mix in green chiles, corn and ½ cup of the enchilada sauce. Refrigerate remaining enchilada sauce.

2 Cover; cook on Low heat setting 6 to 7 hours.

3 Remove chicken from slow cooker to plate. Shred chicken using 2 forks; return chicken to slow cooker. Stir in onions. Cover; cook 15 minutes longer.

4 Heat remaining enchilada sauce. Spoon chicken mixture into warmed taco shells; top with lettuce, tomato and warm enchilada sauce.

1 Serving: Calories 290; Total Fat 9g (Saturated Fat 2.5g; Trans Fat 0g); Cholesterol 40mg; Sodium 850mg; Total Carbohydrate 33g (Dietary Fiber 4g); Protein 18g
Exchanges: 1 Starch, 1 Other Carbohydrate, 1 Vegetable, 2 Lean Meat, ½ Fat
Carbohydrate Choices: 2

chicken and pinto tostadas

Prep Time: 15 Minutes • **Start to Finish:** 8 Hours 30 Minutes • 8 servings

1¼ lb boneless skinless chicken thighs

½ cup chunky-style salsa

¼ cup water

2 tablespoons taco seasoning mix (from 1-oz package)

1 can (15 oz) pinto beans, drained, rinsed

8 tostada shells (from 4.5-oz box), heated as directed on box

1 cup shredded lettuce

½ cup sour cream

½ cup refrigerated guacamole (from 12-oz container)

1 Spray 3½- to 4-quart slow cooker with cooking spray. Place chicken in slow cooker. In small bowl, mix salsa, water and taco seasoning mix; pour over chicken.

2 Cover; cook on Low heat setting 8 to 10 hours.

3 Remove chicken from slow cooker to plate. Shred chicken, using 2 forks; return chicken to slow cooker. Stir in beans. Increase heat setting to High. Cover; cook 15 to 20 minutes or until thoroughly heated.

4 Spoon chicken and bean mixture evenly onto warmed tostada shells. Top with lettuce, sour cream and guacamole.

1 Serving: Calories 290; Total Fat 13g (Saturated Fat 4.5g; Trans Fat 0g); Cholesterol 55mg; Sodium 570mg; Total Carbohydrate 24g (Dietary Fiber 5g); Protein 20g **Exchanges:** 1½ Starch, 2 Lean Meat, 1 Fat **Carbohydrate Choices:** 1½

swap it out

If you don't have tostada shells, just break taco shells in half. Place the halves on each plate, and top with the chicken and bean mixture.

big and spicy chicken hoagies

Prep Time: 15 Minutes　•　**Start to Finish:** 6 Hours 15 Minutes　•　8 hoagies

3　tablespoons Caribbean jerk seasoning (dry)

3　lb boneless skinless chicken thighs

1　large red or green bell pepper, chopped (1½ cups)

1　large onion, chopped (1 cup)

½　cup chicken broth

¼　cup ketchup

8　hoagie buns (7 to 8 inch), split

1　Spray 3½- to 4-quart slow cooker with cooking spray. Rub jerk seasoning generously over chicken. Place bell pepper and onion in slow cooker; top with chicken. In small bowl, mix broth and ketchup; pour over chicken.

2　Cover; cook on Low heat setting 6 to 8 hours.

3　Remove chicken from slow cooker to plate. Shred chicken using 2 forks. Return chicken to slow cooker; mix well. Use slotted spoon to spoon chicken mixture into buns.

1 Hoagie: Calories 550; Total Fat 13g (Saturated Fat 3.5g, Trans Fat 1g); Cholesterol 110mg; Sodium 1070mg; Total Carbohydrate 60g (Dietary Fiber 3g); Protein 47g **Exchanges:** 3 Starch, 1 Other Carbohydrate, 5½ Very Lean Meat, 1½ Fat **Carbohydrate Choices:** 4

a new twist

This chicken mixture is also delicious served in flour tortillas, topped with sliced avocado, chopped green onions and a sprinkle of Monterey Jack cheese!

tuscan-style chicken sandwiches

Prep Time: 15 Minutes • **Start to Finish:** 6 Hours 15 Minutes • 6 sandwiches

1¼ lb boneless skinless chicken thighs

2 cloves garlic, finely chopped

½ cup roasted red bell peppers (from a jar), drained, cut into bite-size strips

½ teaspoon salt

¼ cup mayonnaise

3 tablespoons basil pesto

1 focaccia bread (10 to 12 inch)

6 slices tomato

1 Spray 3½- to 4-quart slow cooker with cooking spray. Place chicken in slow cooker; sprinkle with garlic, roasted peppers and salt.

2 Cover; cook on Low heat setting 6 to 7 hours.

3 Remove chicken from slow cooker to plate. Shred chicken using 2 forks; return to slow cooker and mix well.

4 In small bowl, mix mayonnaise and pesto. Cut focaccia bread into 6 wedges; cut each wedge in half horizontally. Spread cut sides with mayonnaise mixture. With slotted spoon, place about ⅓ cup chicken mixture on each bread bottom; top each with tomato slice. Cover with bread tops.

1 Sandwich: Calories 640; Total Fat 26g (Saturated Fat 5g, Trans Fat 0g); Cholesterol 65mg; Sodium 1670mg; Total Carbohydrate 70g (Dietary Fiber 3g); Protein 31g **Exchanges:** 3½ Starch, 1 Other Carbohydrate, 3 Very Lean Meat, 4½ Fat **Carbohydrate Choices:** 4½

buffalo chicken sandwiches

Prep Time: 30 Minutes • **Start to Finish:** 7 Hours 30 Minutes • 12 sandwiches

3 to 3¼ lb boneless skinless chicken thighs

1¾ cups Buffalo wing sauce

1 English (hothouse) cucumber

12 large burger buns, split

¾ cup crumbled blue cheese (3 oz)

1 Spray 3½- to 4-quart slow cooker with cooking spray. Place chicken in slow cooker. Pour 1 cup of the Buffalo wing sauce over chicken. Cover; cook on Low heat setting 7 to 8 hours.

2 Remove chicken from slow cooker to medium bowl. Place strainer over another medium bowl. Pour juices from slow cooker through strainer into bowl; skim fat. Reserve 1½ cups juices. Stir chicken to separate into pieces; return chicken to slow cooker. Stir in reserved juices. Increase heat setting to High. Cover; cook about 15 minutes or until thoroughly heated.

3 Meanwhile, cut cucumber in half crosswise. With vegetable peeler, cut 1 strip of peel lengthwise from 1 cucumber half; discard strip that is mostly peel. Continue cutting thin strips lengthwise from cucumber, making about 18 strips. Repeat with other half of cucumber.

4 Fill each bun with ½ cup chicken mixture, about 3 strips of cucumber, 1 tablespoon of the remaining Buffalo wing sauce and 1 tablespoon blue cheese.

1 Sandwich: Calories 400; Total Fat 15g (Saturated Fat 5g; Trans Fat 0.5g); Cholesterol 85mg; Sodium 1390mg; Total Carbohydrate 31g (Dietary Fiber 1g); Protein 34g **Exchanges:** 2 Starch, 4 Lean Meat, ½ Fat **Carbohydrate Choices:** 2

a new twist

To make a quick and delicious appetizer, fill frozen mini fillo shells with the chicken mixture, and top with finely chopped celery and a dollop of creamy blue cheese or ranch dressing.

buffalo chicken wraps

Prep Time: 10 Minutes • **Start to Finish:** 6 Hours 10 Minutes • 8 servings

2 lb boneless skinless chicken thighs

½ teaspoon salt

¾ cup Buffalo wing sauce

¾ cup ranch dressing

1 package (11 oz) flour tortillas for burritos (8 tortillas; 8 inch), heated as directed on package

3 cups shredded lettuce

1 Spray 1½-quart slow cooker with cooking spray. Place chicken in slow cooker; sprinkle with salt.

2 Cover; cook on Low heat setting 6 to 7 hours.

3 With slotted spoon, remove chicken from slow cooker to plate; discard liquid in slow cooker. In slow cooker, mix Buffalo wing sauce and ¼ cup of the ranch dressing. Shred chicken using 2 forks; return chicken to slow cooker. Stir gently to mix with sauce.

4 To serve, spread each warmed tortilla with 1 tablespoon remaining ranch dressing; top each with about ½ cup chicken mixture and about ⅓ cup lettuce. Roll up tortilla; secure with toothpicks.

1 Serving: Calories 450; Total Fat 24g (Saturated Fat 6g; Trans Fat 0g); Cholesterol 80mg; Sodium 940mg; Total Carbohydrate 31g (Dietary Fiber 0g); Protein 27g **Exchanges:** 2 Starch, 3 Lean Meat, 3 Fat **Carbohydrate Choices:** 2

swap it out

Blue cheese dressing also pairs well with this Buffalo chicken mixture in place of the ranch dressing.

chicken verde tortilla soup

Prep Time: 15 Minutes • **Start to Finish:** 5 Hours 15 Minutes • 6 servings (1½ cups each)

6 boneless skinless chicken thighs (about 1¼ lb)

1 medium onion, chopped (½ cup)

3 soft corn tortillas (6 inch), cut into 1-inch pieces

1½ cups frozen corn (from 12-oz bag), thawed

1 can (15 oz) garbanzo beans, drained, rinsed

1 can (4.5 oz) chopped green chiles

¾ cup green tomatillo salsa (salsa verde)

3½ cups chicken broth

1 teaspoon dried oregano leaves

1 teaspoon ground cumin

½ teaspoon ground red pepper (cayenne)

2 medium tomatoes, seeded, chopped

Chopped fresh cilantro, if desired

1 Spray 3½- to 4-quart slow cooker with cooking spray. In slow cooker, mix all ingredients except tomatoes and cilantro.

2 Cover; cook on Low heat setting 5 to 7 hours.

3 Stir to break up chicken. Stir in tomatoes just before serving. Garnish individual servings with cilantro.

1 Serving: Calories 330; Total Fat 9g (Saturated Fat 2.5g; Trans Fat 0g); Cholesterol 45mg; Sodium 1160mg; Total Carbohydrate 37g (Dietary Fiber 7g); Protein 26g **Exchanges:** 1½ Starch, ½ Other Carbohydrate, 1 Vegetable, 3 Lean Meat **Carbohydrate Choices:** 2½

mexican fire-roasted tomato-chicken soup

Prep Time: 20 Minutes • **Start to Finish:** 5 Hours 20 Minutes • 7 servings (1¼ cups each)

1 lb boneless skinless chicken thighs

1 carton (32 oz) chicken broth (4 cups)

2 cups frozen corn (from 12-oz bag)

1 can (14.5 oz) fire-roasted diced tomatoes, undrained

1 can (15 oz) black beans, drained, rinsed

1 medium red bell pepper, chopped

1 medium onion, chopped (½ cup)

9 soft corn tortillas (6 inch), cut into ½-inch-wide strips

1 tablespoon chili powder

1 teaspoon ground cumin

1 teaspoon salt

¼ teaspoon ground red pepper (cayenne)

¼ cup chopped fresh cilantro

2 tablespoons vegetable oil

Lime wedges, if desired

Chopped avocado, if desired

1 Spray 3- to 4-quart slow cooker with cooking spray. In slow cooker, mix chicken, broth, corn, tomatoes, black beans, bell pepper, onion, tortilla strips from 6 of the tortillas, the chili powder, cumin, salt, red pepper and cilantro.

2 Cover; cook on Low heat setting 5 to 7 hours (or on High heat setting 3 to 4 hours).

3 Remove chicken from slow cooker to plate. Shred chicken using 2 forks; return chicken to slow cooker. Stir in cilantro.

4 In 9-inch nonstick skillet, heat oil over medium heat. Cook remaining tortilla strips in oil 3 to 5 minutes, stirring occasionally, until crisp and light golden brown. Top individual servings of soup with tortilla strips. Garnish with lime wedges and avocado.

1 Serving: Calories 350; Total Fat 11g (Saturated Fat 2.5g; Trans Fat 0g); Cholesterol 40mg; Sodium 1170mg; Total Carbohydrate 41g (Dietary Fiber 9g); Protein 22g **Exchanges:** 1½ Starch, ½ Other Carbohydrate, 1½ Vegetable, 2 Lean Meat, 1 Fat **Carbohydrate Choices:** 3

swap it out

Fire-roasted tomatoes add a subtle smoky flavor to the chili. Regular diced tomatoes can be substituted if you have those on hand instead.

chicken and gnocchi soup

Prep Time: 20 Minutes • **Start to Finish:** 8 Hours 50 Minutes • 6 servings (1½ cups each)

1¼ lb boneless skinless chicken thighs, cut into ¾-inch pieces

1 cup julienne carrots (1½x¼x¼-inch pieces)

1 medium stalk of celery, chopped (½ cup)

1 medium onion, chopped (½ cup)

1 teaspoon dried thyme leaves

1 carton (32 oz) chicken broth (4 cups)

1 can (10¾ oz) condensed cream of mushroom with roasted garlic soup

1 package (16 oz) shelf-stable gnocchi (not frozen or refrigerated)

1 box (9 oz) frozen baby sweet peas, thawed

1 In 10-inch nonstick skillet over medium-high heat, cook chicken 5 to 7 minutes, stirring frequently, until browned.

2 Spray 3½- to 4-quart slow cooker with cooking spray. In slow cooker, mix chicken, carrots, celery, onion, thyme, broth and soup.

3 Cover; cook on Low heat setting 8 to 10 hours.

4 Increase heat setting to High. Stir in gnocchi and peas. Cover; cook about 30 minutes or until gnocchi and peas are tender.

1 Serving: Calories 390; Total Fat 12g (Saturated Fat 3.5g; Trans Fat 0g); Cholesterol 60mg; Sodium 1390mg; Total Carbohydrate 43g (Dietary Fiber 4g); Protein 28g **Exchanges:** 2 Starch, 1 Other Carbohydrate, 3 Lean Meat **Carbohydrate Choices:** 3

swap it out

Plain cream of mushroom or cream of chicken soup will work in this recipe, but the roasted garlic variety adds lots of flavor.

italian chicken-lentil soup

Prep Time: 20 Minutes • **Start to Finish:** 5 Hours 35 Minutes • 6 servings

1 medium onion, chopped (½ cup)

1 medium zucchini, chopped (2 cups)

4 medium carrots, sliced (2 cups)

1 cup dried lentils (8 oz), sorted, rinsed

4½ cups chicken broth

½ teaspoon salt

¼ teaspoon pepper

1 lb boneless skinless chicken thighs

1 cup sliced fresh mushrooms (3 oz)

1 can (28 oz) diced tomatoes, undrained

¼ cup chopped fresh or 1 tablespoon dried basil leaves

Shredded Parmesan cheese, if desired

1 Spray 3½- to 4-quart slow cooker with cooking spray. In slow cooker, mix onion, zucchini, carrots, lentils, broth, salt and pepper. Top with chicken.

2 Cover; cook on Low heat setting 5 to 6 hours.

3 Remove chicken from slow cooker to plate. Shred chicken using 2 forks; return chicken to slow cooker. Stir in mushrooms and tomatoes. Cover; cook about 15 minutes longer or until thoroughly heated.

4 Top individual servings with basil and cheese.

1 Serving: Calories 310; Total Fat 8g (Saturated Fat 2.5g; Trans Fat 0g); Cholesterol 45mg; Sodium 1220mg; Total Carbohydrate 31g (Dietary Fiber 8g); Protein 30g **Exchanges:** 1½ Starch, ½ Other Carbohydrate, 3½ Very Lean Meat, 1 Fat **Carbohydrate Choices:** 2

italian chicken-pasta soup

Prep Time: 15 Minutes • **Start to Finish:** 8 Hours 15 Minutes • 6 servings

1¼ lb boneless skinless chicken thighs, cut into 1-inch pieces

1 cup diced carrots (about 2 medium)

1 medium onion, chopped (½ cup)

½ cup halved pitted ripe olives

2 cloves garlic, finely chopped

1 carton (32 oz) chicken broth (4 cups)

1 can (14.5 oz) Italian-style diced tomatoes, undrained

½ cup uncooked small pasta shells (2 oz)

1 Spray 3½- to 4-quart slow cooker with cooking spray. In slow cooker, mix all ingredients except pasta.

2 Cover; cook on Low heat setting 8 to 10 hours.

3 About 30 minutes before serving, stir in pasta. Increase heat setting to High. Cover; cook 20 to 30 minutes or until pasta is tender.

1 Serving: Calories 230; Total Fat 7g (Saturated Fat 2g, Trans Fat 0g); Cholesterol 60mg; Sodium 830mg; Total Carbohydrate 17g (Dietary Fiber 2g); Protein 23g **Exchanges:** 1 Starch, 1 Vegetable, 2 ½ Very Lean Meat, 1 Fat **Carbohydrate Choices:** 1

make-ahead

The night before, cut up all the ingredients for this slow cooker soup. Package them separately and refrigerate. In the morning, it's easy to assemble the soup in minutes.

chicken and vegetables with dumplings

Prep Time: 10 Minutes • **Start to Finish:** 9 Hours 55 Minutes • 8 servings

2½ to 3 lb boneless skinless chicken thighs

1 lb small red potatoes (about 2½ inches in diameter)

¾ cup coarsely chopped onion

2 cups ready-to-eat baby-cut carrots

3 cans (14 oz each) chicken broth

2 cups Original Bisquick™ mix

½ cup water

2 teaspoons parsley flakes

1 Spray 6-quart slow cooker with cooking spray. In slow cooker, place chicken, potatoes, onion and carrots. Pour broth over ingredients.

2 Cover; cook on Low heat setting 9 to 10 hours.

3 Increase heat setting to High. In medium bowl, stir together baking mix, water and parsley. Drop dough by rounded tablespoonfuls onto hot chicken mixture. Cover; cook 45 to 50 minutes or until dumplings are dry in center.

1 Serving: Calories 420; Total Fat 16g (Saturated Fat 5g; Trans Fat 1g); Cholesterol 90mg; Sodium 970mg; Total Carbohydrate 34g (Dietary Fiber 3g); Protein 35g **Exchanges:** 2 Starch, 1 Vegetable, 4 Lean Meat, ½ Fat **Carbohydrate Choices:** 2

creamy roasted garlic chicken

Prep Time: 15 Minutes • **Start to Finish:** 3 Hours 55 Minutes • 4 servings

1 medium onion, halved, cut into thin slices

1 cut-up whole chicken (3½ to 4 lb)

1 pouch (9 oz) creamy roasted garlic cooking sauce

1½ teaspoons dried thyme leaves

2 tablespoons all-purpose flour

Salt, if desired

Pepper, if desired

1 Spray 5- to 6-quart slow cooker with cooking spray. Place onion in slow cooker. Arrange chicken pieces over onion, in single layer if possible.

2 Reserve ¼ cup of the cooking sauce in small bowl; refrigerate. In separate small bowl, stir together remaining cooking sauce and the thyme with whisk. Pour over chicken.

3 Cover; cook on High heat setting 3 hours 30 minutes (or Low heat setting 6 to 7 hours) or until juice of chicken is clear when thickest pieces are cut to bone (at least 165°F).

4 Remove chicken from slow cooker to plate; cover to keep warm. Add flour to reserved cooking sauce; stir with whisk until blended. Stir into sauce in slow cooker. Cover; cook on High heat setting 10 to 15 minutes or until sauce begins to thicken.

5 Meanwhile, set oven control to broil. Line broiler pan or cookie sheet with foil. Place chicken skin side up on pan. Broil with tops 6 inches from heat 4 to 6 minutes or until golden brown. Serve chicken with sauce. Season to taste with salt and pepper.

1 Serving: Calories 350; Total Fat 14g (Saturated Fat 4g; Trans Fat 0g); Cholesterol 140mg; Sodium 360mg; Total Carbohydrate 8g (Dietary Fiber 0g); Protein 47g
Exchanges: ½ Other Carbohydrate, 7 Very Lean Meat, 2 Fat **Carbohydrate Choices:** ½

chicken pot roast dinner

Prep Time: 10 Minutes • **Start to Finish:** 8 Hours 25 Minutes • 6 servings (1½ cups each)

1 lb small red potatoes (6 to 8), cut into 1-inch pieces (3 cups)

2 cups ready-to-eat baby-cut carrots

1 cup frozen small whole onions (from 1-lb bag), thawed

6 boneless skinless chicken thighs (about 1¼ lb)

½ teaspoon salt

⅛ teaspoon pepper

1 jar (12 oz) chicken gravy

1½ cups frozen sweet peas (from 12-oz bag), thawed

1 Spray 3½- to 4-quart slow cooker with cooking spray. In slow cooker, place potatoes, carrots and onions. Sprinkle chicken with salt and pepper; place over vegetables. Pour gravy over top.

2 Cover; cook on Low heat setting 8 to 10 hours.

3 Increase heat setting to High. Stir in peas. Cover; cook about 15 minutes or until peas are tender.

1 Serving: Calories 310; Total Fat 11g (Saturated Fat 3g; Trans Fat 0g); Cholesterol 60mg; Sodium 630mg; Total Carbohydrate 28g (Dietary Fiber 4g); Protein 24g **Exchanges:** 1½ Starch, 1½ Vegetable, 2½ Lean Meat, ½ Fat **Carbohydrate Choices:** 2

spanish chicken

Prep Time: 15 Minutes ● **Start to Finish:** 6 Hours 15 Minutes ● 6 servings

1¾ lb boneless skinless chicken breasts or thighs, cut into 1-inch pieces

1 lb Italian turkey sausage, cut into 1-inch slices

1 large red bell pepper, chopped (1½ cups)

1 large onion, chopped (1 cup)

2 cloves garlic, finely chopped

1 teaspoon dried oregano leaves

½ to 1 teaspoon crushed red pepper flakes

1 can (28 oz) diced tomatoes, undrained

1 can (6 oz) tomato paste

1 can (14 oz) quartered artichoke hearts, drained

1 can (3.8 oz) sliced ripe olives, drained

2 cups hot cooked rice

1 Spray 3½- to 4-quart slow cooker with cooking spray. In slow cooker, mix all ingredients except artichoke hearts, olives and rice.

2 Cover; cook on Low heat setting 6 to 8 hours.

3 Stir artichoke hearts and olives into mixture in slow cooker. Cover; heat until hot. Serve with rice.

1 Serving: Calories 490; Total Fat 14g (Saturated Fat 3.5g; Trans Fat 0g); Cholesterol 120mg; Sodium 1860mg; Total Carbohydrate 46g (Dietary Fiber 8g); Protein 47g
Exchanges: 3 Starch, 5 Very Lean Meat, 1 Fat **Carbohydrate Choices:** 3

mediterranean chicken marbella

Prep Time: 15 Minutes • **Start to Finish:** 9 Hours 30 Minutes • 8 servings

¼ cup packed brown sugar

2 teaspoons dried oregano leaves

1 teaspoon salt

¼ teaspoon pepper

3 cloves garlic, finely chopped

⅓ cup white wine or chicken broth

2 tablespoons red wine vinegar

2½ lb boneless skinless chicken thighs

2 dried bay leaves

½ cup pimiento-stuffed green olives

½ cup pitted bite-size dried plums (from 12-oz package)

½ cup roasted red bell peppers (from 7-oz jar), drained, coarsely chopped

2 tablespoons capers, drained

1 box (10 oz) couscous

¼ cup chopped fresh parsley

1 In large bowl, mix brown sugar, oregano, salt, pepper, garlic, wine and vinegar. Add chicken; turn to coat well. Add bay leaves. Cover; refrigerate at least 4 hours or overnight to marinate.

2 Spray 3- to 4-quart slow cooker with cooking spray. In slow cooker, place chicken and marinade mixture.

3 Cover; cook on Low heat setting 5 to 6 hours.

4 Stir olives, plums, roasted peppers and capers into chicken mixture in slow cooker. Cover; cook about 15 minutes longer or until hot. Meanwhile, cook couscous as directed on package.

5 Transfer chicken with juices to large serving bowl or deep platter; remove bay leaves. Sprinkle parsley over chicken mixture. Serve with couscous.

1 Serving: Calories 430; Total Fat 13g (Saturated Fat 4g; Trans Fat 0g); Cholesterol 85mg; Sodium 640mg; Total Carbohydrate 43g (Dietary Fiber 3g); Protein 35g **Exchanges:** 2 Starch, 1 Other Carbohydrate, 4 Lean Meat **Carbohydrate Choices:** 3

salsa chicken

Prep Time: 10 Minutes • **Start to Finish:** 7 Hours 10 Minutes • 4 servings

8 boneless skinless chicken thighs

1 teaspoon salt

1 tablespoon vegetable oil

½ cup chunky-style salsa

1 can (15 oz) black beans, drained, rinsed

1 can (11 oz) whole kernel sweet corn, drained

1 or 2 boxes (8 oz each) seasoned yellow rice mix with saffron, if desired

2 tablespoons chopped fresh cilantro

1 Sprinkle chicken with salt. In 12-inch skillet, heat oil over medium-high heat. Cook chicken in oil about 4 minutes, turning once, until browned.

2 Spray 3½- to 5-quart slow cooker with cooking spray. In slow cooker, mix salsa, beans and corn. Top with chicken.

3 Cover; cook on Low heat setting 7 to 9 hours.

4 About 30 minutes before serving, cook rice mix as directed on package. Serve chicken mixture with rice. Sprinkle with cilantro.

1 Serving: Calories 460; Total Fat 15g (Saturated Fat 4g; Trans Fat 0g); Cholesterol 120mg; Sodium 1040mg; Total Carbohydrate 33g (Dietary Fiber 9g); Protein 49g **Exchanges:** 2 Starch, 1 Vegetable, 2 Very Lean Meat, 4 Lean Meat **Carbohydrate Choices:** 2

a new twist

Turn leftovers into burritos topped with sour cream or guacamole and extra salsa.

swap it out

Substitute a can of corn with red and green peppers for the regular corn to add a bit of extra color.

green chile–chicken enchilada casserole

Prep Time: 20 Minutes • **Start to Finish:** 6 Hours 25 Minutes • 6 servings

2 cans (4.5 oz each) chopped green chiles

1 can (10¾ oz) condensed cream of chicken soup

1 can (10 oz) green enchilada sauce

¼ cup mayonnaise or salad dressing

12 soft corn tortillas (6 inch), cut into ¾-inch strips

3 cups shredded cooked chicken

1 can (15 oz) black beans, drained, rinsed

2 cups shredded Mexican cheese blend (8 oz)

2 large tomatoes, chopped (about 2 cups)

2 cups chopped lettuce

½ cup sour cream

1 Spray 3½- to 4-quart slow cooker with cooking spray. In slow cooker, spread 1 can green chiles. In medium bowl, mix remaining can of green chiles, the soup, enchilada sauce and mayonnaise.

2 Arrange one-third of the tortilla strips over chiles in slow cooker. Top with 1 cup of the chicken, ½ cup of the beans, ½ cup of the cheese and 1 cup of the enchilada sauce mixture, spreading to edge of slow cooker to completely cover tortilla strips. Repeat layers twice, reserving last ½ cup of cheese.

3 Cover; cook on Low heat setting 6 to 7 hours.

4 Sprinkle remaining ½ cup cheese over casserole. Cover; cook about 5 minutes longer or until cheese is melted. Serve with tomatoes, lettuce and sour cream.

1 Serving: Calories 630; Total Fat 32g (Saturated Fat 13g; Trans Fat 0.5g); Cholesterol 115mg; Sodium 1240mg; Total Carbohydrate 48g (Dietary Fiber 9g); Protein 39g **Exchanges:** 2 Starch, 1½ Other Carbohydrate, 4½ Lean Meat, 3 Fat **Carbohydrate Choices:** 3

thai peanut chicken

Prep Time: 10 Minutes • **Start to Finish:** 5 Hours 10 Minutes • 6 servings

2 lb boneless skinless chicken thighs

1 bottle (13.5 oz) Thai peanut sauce

2 medium carrots, sliced (¾ cup)

4 medium green onions, sliced (¼ cup)

1 cup uncooked regular long-grain white rice

2¼ cups water

¼ cup chopped cocktail peanuts

2 tablespoons chopped fresh cilantro

½ cup chopped red bell pepper, if desired

1 Spray 3½- to 4-quart slow cooker with cooking spray. Place chicken in slow cooker. In medium bowl, mix peanut sauce, carrots and onions; pour over chicken.

2 Cover; cook on Low heat setting 5 to 6 hours.

3 About 30 minutes before serving, cook rice in water as directed on package; spoon rice onto serving plate or into bowl. With slotted spoon, remove chicken from slow cooker; arrange over rice. Pour sauce from slow cooker over chicken. Sprinkle with peanuts, cilantro and bell pepper.

1 Serving: Calories 490; Total Fat 21g (Saturated Fat 3g; Trans Fat 0g); Cholesterol 60mg; Sodium 1370mg; Total Carbohydrate 46g (Dietary Fiber 1g); Protein 29g **Exchanges:** 2 Starch, 1 Other Carbohydrate, 3 Lean Meat, 2 Fat **Carbohydrate Choices:** 3

chicken chow mein

Prep Time: 25 Minutes • **Start to Finish:** 6 Hours 40 Minutes • 4 servings

1 tablespoon vegetable oil

1½ lb boneless skinless chicken thighs or breasts, cut into 1-inch pieces

2 medium carrots, sliced diagonally (1 cup)

2 medium stalks celery, coarsely chopped (1 cup)

1 medium onion, chopped (½ cup)

2 cloves garlic, finely chopped

1 can (8 oz) sliced water chestnuts, drained

1 cup chicken broth

2 tablespoons soy sauce

½ teaspoon finely chopped gingerroot

2 tablespoons cornstarch

3 tablespoons cold water

1 cup sliced fresh mushrooms (3 oz)

1 cup fresh snow pea pods (4 oz)

Chow mein noodles, if desired

1 In 10-inch skillet, heat oil over medium-high heat. Cook chicken in oil about 5 minutes, turning once, until browned.

2 Spray 3½- to 6-quart slow cooker with cooking spray. In slow cooker, place carrots, celery, onion, garlic and water chestnuts; top with chicken. In small bowl, mix broth, soy sauce and gingerroot; pour over chicken.

3 Cover; cook on Low heat setting 6 to 8 hours.

4 In small bowl, mix cornstarch and water until smooth; stir into chicken mixture in slow cooker. Stir in mushrooms and pea pods. Increase heat setting to High. Cover; cook 15 minutes. Serve with chow mein noodles.

1 Serving: Calories 260; Total Fat 9g (Saturated Fat 2.5g; Trans Fat 0g); Cholesterol 60mg; Sodium 810mg; Total Carbohydrate 19g (Dietary Fiber 4g); Protein 25g **Exchanges:** 3 Vegetable, 3 Lean Meat, ½ Fat **Carbohydrate Choices:** 1

mango chutney chicken curry

Prep Time: 20 Minutes • **Start to Finish:** 6 Hours 20 Minutes • 4 servings

4 bone-in chicken breasts (about 3 lb), skin removed

1 can (15 oz) garbanzo beans, drained, rinsed

1 small onion, thinly sliced

1 small red bell pepper, chopped (½ cup)

1 cup fresh sugar snap peas

¾ cup water

2 tablespoons cornstarch

1½ teaspoons curry powder

¼ teaspoon salt

¼ teaspoon pepper

1 jar (9 oz) mango chutney

4 cups hot cooked rice or couscous

1 Spray 3½- to 4-quart slow cooker with cooking spray. In slow cooker, layer chicken, beans, onion, bell pepper and peas.

2 In medium bowl, mix water, cornstarch, curry powder, salt, pepper and chutney. Pour over ingredients in slow cooker.

3 Cover; cook on Low heat setting 6 to 7 hours. Serve chicken and vegetables over rice.

1 Serving: Calories 610; Total Fat 7g (Saturated Fat 1.5g; Trans Fat 0g); Cholesterol 75mg; Sodium 380mg; Total Carbohydrate 97g (Dietary Fiber 7g); Protein 39g **Exchanges:** 3½ Starch, 2 Other Carbohydrate, 2½ Vegetable, 3½ Very Lean Meat, ½ Fat **Carbohydrate Choices:** 6½

saucy orange barbecued chicken

Prep Time: 15 Minutes • **Start to Finish:** 6 Hours 30 Minutes • 4 servings

1 tablespoon vegetable oil

3 lb bone-in chicken thighs, skin removed

¾ cup chili sauce

⅓ cup orange marmalade

1 tablespoon packed brown sugar

1 tablespoon Dijon mustard

1 tablespoon red wine vinegar

1 teaspoon Worcestershire sauce

1 Spray 4-quart slow cooker with cooking spray. In 12-inch nonstick skillet, heat oil over medium-high heat. Cook chicken in oil 8 to 10 minutes, turning occasionally, until browned on both sides. Place chicken in slow cooker.

2 Cover; cook on Low heat setting 6 to 7 hours or until chicken is tender.

3 About 30 minutes before serving, in 1-quart saucepan, stir together remaining ingredients. Cook over medium heat 10 to 15 minutes, stirring occasionally, until thickened.

4 Drain excess liquid from slow cooker. Pour sauce over chicken. Cover; cook 10 to 15 minutes longer.

1 Serving: Calories 690; Total Fat 31g (Saturated Fat 9g; Trans Fat 0.5g); Cholesterol 210mg; Sodium 990mg; Total Carbohydrate 32g (Dietary Fiber 3g); Protein 72g
Exchanges: 2 Other Carbohydrate, 10 Lean Meat **Carbohydrate Choices:** 2

swap it out

Substitute your favorite preserves, such as plum or even raspberry, for the orange marmalade.

spicy asian barbecued drummettes

Prep Time: 15 Minutes • **Start to Finish:** 3 Hours 15 Minutes • 4 servings

3 lb chicken wing drummettes (about 20)

½ teaspoon salt

¼ teaspoon pepper

1 cup honey barbecue sauce

1 tablespoon Sriracha sauce

1 tablespoon soy sauce

3 cloves garlic, finely chopped

Toasted sesame seed, if desired

Sliced green onions, if desired

1 Set oven control to broil. Spray 3½- to 4-quart slow cooker with cooking spray. Spray broiler pan rack with cooking spray. Sprinkle drummettes with salt and pepper. Place on rack in pan.

2 Broil 3 inches from heat 8 minutes or until browned. Place drummettes in slow cooker. In small bowl, mix barbecue sauce, Sriracha sauce, soy sauce and garlic; pour over drummettes.

3 Cover; cook on Low heat setting 3 hours. Serve with sauce for dipping. Garnish with sesame seed and onions.

1 Serving: Calories 380; Total Fat 19g (Saturated Fat 5g; Trans Fat 0g); Cholesterol 0mg; Sodium 1510mg; Total Carbohydrate 28g (Dietary Fiber 0g); Protein 23g **Exchanges:** 1½ Other Carbohydrate, 3 Medium-Fat Meat, ½ Fat **Carbohydrate Choices:** 1½

mole chicken wings

Prep Time: 25 Minutes • **Start to Finish:** 3 Hours 25 Minutes • 12 servings (about 2 wings each)

CHICKEN

- 3 lb chicken wingettes and drummettes
- ½ teaspoon kosher (coarse) salt
- ¼ teaspoon pepper

GLAZE

- 2 chipotle chiles in adobo sauce (from 7-oz can), finely chopped
- 1 can (14.5 oz) fire-roasted diced tomatoes, well drained
- 2 tablespoons chopped onion
- 3 tablespoons honey
- 1 oz bittersweet baking chocolate, chopped (about 2 tablespoons)
- 1 tablespoon tomato paste
- ½ teaspoon ground cinnamon
- ½ teaspoon ground cumin
- ½ teaspoon kosher (coarse) salt
- 2 cloves garlic, finely chopped

GARNISH

- 3 tablespoons roasted salted pepitas (pumpkin seeds)
- 1 lime, cut into wedges

1 Spray 3½- to 4-quart slow cooker with cooking spray. Set oven control to broil. Spray broiler pan rack with cooking spray. Sprinkle chicken with ½ teaspoon salt and the pepper; place on rack in pan.

2 Broil with tops 3 inches from heat 10 to 12 minutes or until browned, turning once. Place chicken in slow cooker.

3 In food processor, place glaze ingredients. Cover; process about 30 seconds or until smooth. Pour glaze over chicken; stir to coat.

4 Cover; cook on Low heat setting 3 hours. Remove chicken from slow cooker; spoon glaze from slow cooker into bowl for dipping. Garnish with pepitas and lime wedges.

1 Serving: Calories 180; Total Fat 10g (Saturated Fat 3g; Trans Fat 0g); Cholesterol 35mg; Sodium 280mg; Total Carbohydrate 9g (Dietary Fiber 1g); Protein 12g **Exchanges:** ½ Other Carbohydrate, 2 Medium-Fat Meat **Carbohydrate Choices:** ½

CHAPTER 6

Almost No Cooking

asian chicken salad lettuce cups

Prep Time: 15 Minutes • **Start to Finish:** 15 Minutes • 24 servings

2 cups finely chopped cooked chicken

4 medium green onions, diagonally sliced (¼ cup)

1 can (8 oz) sliced water chestnuts, drained, finely chopped

½ cup spicy peanut sauce (from 7-oz bottle)

1 tablespoon chopped fresh mint leaves

¼ teaspoon crushed red pepper flakes

24 small (about 3 inch) Bibb lettuce leaves (about 1½ heads), breaking larger leaves into smaller size

½ cup chopped roasted salted peanuts

1 In medium bowl, mix chicken, onions, water chestnuts, peanut sauce, mint and pepper flakes.

2 Spoon about 2 tablespoons chicken mixture onto each lettuce leaf. Sprinkle with peanuts.

1 Serving: Calories 60; Total Fat 3.5g (Saturated Fat 0.5g; Trans Fat 0g); Cholesterol 10mg; Sodium 35mg; Total Carbohydrate 2g (Dietary Fiber 0g); Protein 5g **Exchanges:** ½ Lean Meat, ½ Fat **Carbohydrate Choices:** 0

chopped asian salad

Prep Time: 25 Minutes • **Start to Finish:** 25 Minutes • 4 servings

LIME DRESSING

- ⅓ cup frozen limeade concentrate, thawed
- ¼ cup vegetable oil
- 1 tablespoon rice vinegar
- 1 teaspoon grated gingerroot
- ¼ teaspoon salt

SALAD

- 2 cups chopped escarole
- 1 cup chopped cooked chicken
- 1 small jicama, peeled, chopped (2 cups)
- 1 large papaya, peeled, seeded and chopped (2 cups)
- 1 large red or yellow bell pepper, chopped (1 cup)
- ½ cup dry-roasted peanuts
- ¼ cup chopped fresh cilantro

1 In tightly covered container, shake dressing ingredients.

2 In large bowl, mix escarole, chicken, jicama, papaya and bell pepper. Pour dressing over salad; toss to coat. Top with peanuts and cilantro.

1 Serving: Calories 440; Total Fat 25g (Saturated Fat 4g; Trans Fat 0g); Cholesterol 30mg; Sodium 250mg; Total Carbohydrate 37g (Dietary Fiber 9g); Protein 16g
Exchanges: 1 Fruit, 1 Other Carbohydrate, 2 Vegetable, 1½ Lean Meat, 4 Fat
Carbohydrate Choices: 2½

a new twist

It's easy to make this a seafood salad. Just use 1 cup cooked small shrimp or crabmeat instead of the chicken.

swap it out

Peaches or nectarines can be used instead of the papaya.

crunchy asian chicken salad

Prep Time: 15 Minutes • **Start to Finish:** 15 Minutes • 6 servings (1¼ cups each)

2   tablespoons butter

1   package (3 oz) oriental-flavor ramen noodle soup mix

2   tablespoons sesame seed

¼   cup sugar

¼   cup white vinegar

1   tablespoon dark sesame oil

½   teaspoon pepper

2   cups cut-up cooked chicken

¼   cup dry-roasted peanuts, if desired

4   medium green onions, sliced (¼ cup)

1   bag (16 oz) coleslaw mix (8 cups)

1   can (11 oz) mandarin orange segments, drained

1 In 10-inch skillet, melt butter over medium heat. Stir in seasoning packet from soup mix. Break block of noodles into bite-size pieces over skillet; stir into butter mixture. Cook 2 minutes, stirring occasionally. Stir in sesame seed. Cook about 2 minutes longer, stirring occasionally, until noodles are golden brown; remove from heat.

2 In large glass or plastic bowl, mix sugar, vinegar, oil and pepper. Add noodle mixture and remaining ingredients; toss. Serve immediately.

1 Serving: Calories 290; Total Fat 13g (Saturated Fat 4g; Trans Fat 1g); Cholesterol 50mg; Sodium 260mg; Total Carbohydrate 26g (Dietary Fiber 3g); Protein 16g **Exchanges:** 1 Starch, 2 Vegetable, 1 Medium-Fat Meat, 1 Fat **Carbohydrate Choices:** 2

thai shredded chicken salad

Prep Time: 15 Minutes • **Start to Finish:** 15 Minutes • 4 servings (1¼ cups each)

SALAD

- 2 cups shredded deli rotisserie chicken (from 2- to 3-lb chicken)
- 1 cup julienne carrots (1½x¼x¼ inch)
- 1 cup broccoli slaw mix
- 1 large green onion, chopped

DRESSING

- 2 tablespoons creamy peanut butter
- 2 tablespoons rice vinegar
- 1 tablespoon vegetable oil
- 1 tablespoon honey
- 4 teaspoons soy sauce
- ⅛ teaspoon red pepper sauce

  Fresh cilantro, if desired

1 In large bowl, toss salad ingredients.

2 In small bowl, beat peanut butter, vinegar, oil, honey, soy sauce and pepper sauce with whisk until well blended. Drizzle dressing over salad; toss until evenly coated. Garnish with cilantro.

1 Serving: Calories 310; Total Fat 17g (Saturated Fat 3.5g; Trans Fat 0g); Cholesterol 60mg; Sodium 710mg; Total Carbohydrate 15g (Dietary Fiber 2g); Protein 22g **Exchanges:** 1 Other Carbohydrate, 3 Lean Meat, 1½ Fat **Carbohydrate Choices:** 1

gazpacho-style chicken salad

Prep Time: 25 Minutes ● **Start to Finish:** 25 Minutes ● 2 servings

4 cups packed torn green and/or red leaf lettuce

1 package (6 oz) refrigerated grilled chicken breast strips

1 medium tomato, chopped (¾ cup)

1 cup chopped peeled cucumber

¾ cup chopped yellow bell pepper

⅓ cup thinly sliced red onion

DRESSING

½ cup spicy Bloody Mary mix

3 tablespoons red wine vinegar

2 tablespoons olive oil

½ teaspoon salt

¼ teaspoon pepper

¼ teaspoon red pepper sauce

1 clove garlic, finely chopped

1 Place lettuce on serving platter. Arrange chicken over lettuce. Place tomato, cucumber, bell pepper and onion on top of lettuce and chicken.

2 In tightly covered container, shake dressing ingredients. Spoon ¼ cup dressing over salad; gently toss to coat. Serve immediately. Reserve remaining dressing for another use.

1 Serving: Calories 240; Total Fat 8g (Saturated Fat 1.5g; Trans Fat 0g); Cholesterol 70mg; Sodium 720mg; Total Carbohydrate 13g (Dietary Fiber 3g); Protein 29g **Exchanges:** 3 Vegetable, 3 Lean Meat **Carbohydrate Choices:** 1

swap it out

Try white wine vinegar or cider vinegar instead of the red wine vinegar.

chipotle chicken taco salads

Prep Time: 20 Minutes • **Start to Finish:** 20 Minutes • 6 servings

DRESSING

- ½ cup ranch dressing
- ½ cup chunky-style salsa
- 2 teaspoons finely chopped chipotle chiles in adobo sauce (from 7-oz can)

SALAD

- 1 bag (9 oz) leafy green romaine lettuce
- 2 cups shredded deli rotisserie chicken
- 1 cup cherry tomato halves
- 1 medium ripe avocado, pitted, peeled and cut into 1-inch pieces
- ½ cup canned whole kernel sweet corn, drained
- ½ cup bite-size pieces thinly sliced red onion
- 6 taco shells (from 4.6-oz box), broken into large pieces or crushed

1 Mix dressing ingredients in small bowl; refrigerate while preparing salad.

2 Divide lettuce among 6 serving plates. Top each with chicken, tomatoes, avocado and corn. Drizzle with dressing; sprinkle with red onion. Serve with or sprinkle with taco shells.

1 Serving: Calories 310; Total Fat 20g (Saturated Fat 4g; Trans Fat 0g); Cholesterol 45mg; Sodium 690mg; Total Carbohydrate 18g (Dietary Fiber 4g); Protein 15g **Exchanges:** 1 Starch, 1 Vegetable, 1 Very Lean Meat, ½ Lean Meat, 3½ Fat **Carbohydrate Choices:** 1

tostada chicken salad

Prep Time: 15 Minutes • **Start to Finish:** 15 Minutes • 2 servings

1 cup shredded cooked chicken

2 tablespoons chopped fresh cilantro

2 tablespoons sour cream

2 tablespoons mayonnaise or salad dressing

2 teaspoons taco seasoning mix (from 1-oz package) or Southwest seasoning (from 1.87-oz jar)

1 medium green onion, chopped (1 tablespoon)

2 tostada shells

3 cups shredded iceberg lettuce

¼ cup chunky-style salsa

½ medium avocado, sliced, if desired

1 In medium bowl, mix chicken, cilantro, sour cream, mayonnaise, taco seasoning mix and onion.

2 Place 1 tostada shell on each serving plate. Top each with half of the lettuce, chicken mixture and salsa. Garnish with avocado.

1 Serving: Calories 340; Total Fat 22g (Saturated Fat 5g; Trans Fat 1.5g); Cholesterol 75mg; Sodium 700mg; Total Carbohydrate 15g (Dietary Fiber 2g); Protein 21g **Exchanges:** ½ Starch, ½ Other Carbohydrate, 2½ Lean Meat, 3 Fat **Carbohydrate Choices:** 1

balsamic-mozzarella chicken salad

Prep Time: 10 Minutes • **Start to Finish:** 10 Minutes • 4 servings (1¼ cups each)

1 container (8 oz) small fresh mozzarella cheese balls, drained

1 pint (2 cups) cherry tomatoes, cut in half

2 packages (6 oz each) refrigerated grilled chicken breast strips

½ cup balsamic vinaigrette dressing

12 leaves romaine lettuce

Chopped fresh basil leaves, if desired

1 In medium bowl, gently stir mozzarella, tomatoes and chicken. Drizzle with dressing; toss lightly.

2 Line each of 4 plates with 3 lettuce leaves; spoon salad onto lettuce-lined plates. Garnish with basil.

1 Serving: Calories 380; Total Fat 23g (Saturated Fat 2.5g; Trans Fat 0g); Cholesterol 95mg; Sodium 980mg; Total Carbohydrate 10g (Dietary Fiber 1g); Protein 32g
Exchanges: ½ Other Carbohydrate, 3 Lean Meat, 1½ Medium-Fat Meat, 1½ Fat
Carbohydrate Choices: ½

a new twist

Add ½ cup chopped fresh basil leaves to the salad rather than just sprinkling some on top.

swap it out

If small fresh mozzarella cheese balls (called pearls, perline or perlini) are unavailable, use any size fresh mozzarella and cut into ½-inch pieces.

mediterranean chicken salad

Prep Time: 30 Minutes • **Start to Finish:** 3 Hours 30 Minutes • 8 servings

½ cup mayonnaise

1½ cups plain yogurt

½ cup fresh basil leaves

2 tablespoons lemon juice

2 cups cubed deli rotisserie chicken (from 2- to 3-lb chicken)

1 cup cubed cooked peeled potatoes

1 medium red bell pepper, chopped (1 cup)

1 medium green bell pepper, chopped (1 cup)

1 medium yellow bell pepper, chopped (1 cup)

½ cup Greek olives, pitted

¼ cup capers, rinsed

¼ cup chopped red onion

Salt and pepper to taste

Mixed salad greens, if desired

1 In food processor, place mayonnaise, ½ cup of the yogurt and the basil. Cover; process until smooth. Add lemon juice. Cover; process just until blended. Transfer mixture to large bowl.

2 Add remaining 1 cup yogurt to mayonnaise mixture; mix well. Fold in chicken, potatoes, bell peppers, olives, capers and onion; season with salt and pepper.

3 Cover; refrigerate 3 hours to blend flavors. Serve salad on mixed greens.

1 Serving: Calories 250; Total Fat 15g (Saturated Fat 2.5g; Trans Fat 0g); Cholesterol 35mg; Sodium 470mg; Total Carbohydrate 16g (Dietary Fiber 2g); Protein 12g **Exchanges:** ½ Starch, ½ Other Carbohydrate, ½ Vegetable, 1 Very Lean Meat, ½ Lean Meat, 2½ Fat **Carbohydrate Choices:** 1

easy club salad

Prep Time: 10 Minutes • **Start to Finish:** 10 Minutes • 4 servings

6 cups bite-size pieces lettuce

1½ cups cut-up cooked chicken

1 medium tomato, cut into eighths

⅓ cup Thousand Island dressing

⅓ cup cooked real bacon bits or pieces (from a jar or package)

Hard-cooked egg slices, if desired

1 In large bowl, toss lettuce, chicken, tomato, dressing and bacon. Garnish with egg slices.

1 Serving: Calories 210; Total Fat 12g (Saturated Fat 2.5g; Trans Fat 0g); Cholesterol 50mg; Sodium 370mg; Total Carbohydrate 7g (Dietary Fiber 2g); Protein 19g **Exchanges:** 1 Vegetable, 2½ Lean Meat, 1 Fat **Carbohydrate Choices:** ½

swap it out

Two 4.5-ounce cans of chunk chicken, drained, can be substituted for the cooked chicken.

curried chicken and grape salad

Prep Time: 30 Minutes • **Start to Finish:** 30 Minutes • 5 servings (1 cup each)

DRESSING

- ½ cup mayonnaise or salad dressing
- 2 tablespoons lemon juice
- 2 to 3 teaspoons curry powder
- ½ teaspoon salt
- ¼ teaspoon pepper

SALAD

- 3 cups diced deli rotisserie chicken (from 2- to 2½-lb chicken)
- 1 cup thinly sliced celery
- 1 cup seedless red grapes, halved
- 3 tablespoons slivered almonds, toasted*

1 In large bowl, stir dressing ingredients until well mixed.

2 Stir in chicken, celery and grapes. Sprinkle with almonds.

*To toast almonds, sprinkle in ungreased skillet. Cook over medium heat 5 to 7 minutes, stirring frequently until nuts begin to brown, then stirring constantly until nuts are light brown.

1 Serving: Calories 270; Total Fat 14g (Saturated Fat 3g; Trans Fat 0g); Cholesterol 80mg; Sodium 860mg; Total Carbohydrate 11g (Dietary Fiber 1g); Protein 25g **Exchanges:** 1 Other Carbohydrate, 3 Lean Meat, ½ Fat **Carbohydrate Choices:** 1

tropical chicken salad

Prep Time: 25 Minutes • **Start to Finish:** 25 Minutes • 4 servings (2 cups each)

4 cups fresh baby spinach leaves

4 cups bite-size pieces romaine lettuce

1 cup fresh pineapple chunks

2 cups chopped deli rotisserie chicken (from 2- to 3-lb chicken)

1 medium red bell pepper, chopped (1 cup)

3 medium green onions, chopped (3 tablespoons)

⅓ cup Italian dressing

3 tablespoons orange marmalade

¼ cup salted cashews

1 On large serving platter or in large bowl, toss spinach and romaine. Top with pineapple, chicken, bell pepper and onions.

2 In small bowl, stir together dressing and orange marmalade. Drizzle dressing over salad. Sprinkle with cashews.

1 Serving: Calories 350; Total Fat 18g (Saturated Fat 3g; Trans Fat 0g); Cholesterol 65mg; Sodium 610mg; Total Carbohydrate 25g (Dietary Fiber 4g); Protein 24g **Exchanges:** 1½ Other Carbohydrate, 1 Vegetable, 3 Lean Meat, 1½ Fat **Carbohydrate Choices:** 1½

layered caribbean chicken salad

Prep Time: 30 Minutes • **Start to Finish:** 30 Minutes • 6 servings (1½ cups each)

DRESSING

- 1 container (6 oz) piña colada fat-free yogurt
- 4½ to 6 teaspoons lime juice
- 1 teaspoon Caribbean jerk seasoning (dry)

SALAD

- 3 cups shredded romaine lettuce
- 2 cups cubed cooked chicken
- 1 cup shredded Monterey Jack cheese (4 oz)
- 1 can (15 oz) black beans, drained, rinsed
- 1½ cups diced peeled ripe mango
- ½ cup chopped seeded plum (Roma) tomatoes (1 to 2 medium)
- 1 cup shredded Cheddar cheese (4 oz)
- 8 medium green onions, thinly sliced (½ cup)
- ½ cup cashews

1 In small bowl, mix dressing ingredients until well blended.

2 In 3- or 4-quart clear glass serving bowl, layer all salad ingredients except cashews in order listed. Spoon dressing over top; sprinkle with cashews.

1 Serving: Calories 450; Total Fat 21g (Saturated Fat 10g; Trans Fat 0g); Cholesterol 80mg; Sodium 320mg; Total Carbohydrate 34g (Dietary Fiber 8g); Protein 31g **Exchanges:** 1 Starch, 1 Other Carbohydrate, 4 Lean Meat, 2 Fat **Carbohydrate Choices:** 2

make-ahead

This salad can be made several hours ahead and refrigerated. Add the cashews just before serving.

summer layered chicken salad

Prep Time: 15 Minutes • **Start to Finish:** 15 Minutes • 6 servings

SALAD

7 cups torn
   romaine lettuce

1 package (9 oz) frozen
   cooked chicken breast
   strips, thawed

½ cup crumbled
   Gorgonzola cheese
   (2 oz)

½ cup pecan halves

1 quart fresh strawberries,
   quartered

DRESSING

2 tablespoons sugar

3 tablespoons red
   wine vinegar

2 tablespoons olive or
   vegetable oil

1 teaspoon Dijon mustard

½ teaspoon salt

1 clove garlic, finely
   chopped

1 In deep 3-quart salad bowl, place half of the lettuce. Layer with chicken, cheese, pecans, remaining lettuce and the strawberries.

2 In small bowl or glass measuring cup, mix dressing ingredients with whisk until well blended. Just before serving, pour dressing over salad.

1 Serving: Calories 240; Total Fat 13g (Saturated Fat 2g; Trans Fat 0g); Cholesterol 35mg; Sodium 470mg; Total Carbohydrate 18g (Dietary Fiber 4g); Protein 14g **Exchanges:** 1 Other Carbohydrate, 2 Very Lean Meat, 2½ Fat **Carbohydrate Choices:** 1

make-ahead

The salad and dressing can be made ahead. Cover each with plastic wrap and refrigerate up to 4 hours before serving.

swap it out

Purchased red wine vinaigrette dressing can be substituted for the homemade dressing.

Easy Cooked Chicken Re-Dos

Start with cubed, shredded or sliced cooked chicken (home-cooked or rotisserie) to make very tasty meals. See Storing Chicken, page 6, and the Cooked Chicken Yields chart, page 7, as guides.

Double-Cheese, Spinach and Chicken Pizza: Heat oven to 425°F. Place 12-inch prebaked original Italian pizza crust (from 14 ounce package) on cookie sheet. Top with ½ cup Alfredo sauce or pizza sauce, 1 cup shredded mozzarella, 2 cups washed fresh baby spinach leaves, 1 cup diced cooked chicken, ¼ cup diced red bell pepper and 1 cup shredded Cheddar cheese.

Chicken Tacos: Mix shredded cooked chicken with enchilada sauce or taco sauce and heat until hot; spoon into taco shells. Top with shredded lettuce, shredded cheese, chopped tomatoes, sliced ripe olives, sour cream and diced avocado.

Chicken-Cashew Wraps: Mix 2 cups shredded cooked chicken, ½ cup each cashew pieces and sliced celery, 2 tablespoons sliced green onions and ⅓ cup honey-mustard salad dressing. Spoon mixture evenly onto 4 (7- to 8-inch) flour tortillas to within 1-inch of edges. Top each evenly with ¼ cup shredded lettuce and 1 tablespoon diced red bell pepper; roll up.

Cherry-Chicken Pitas: Mix 2 cups chopped cooked chicken, ½ cup dried cherries, ½ cup toasted chopped slivered almonds or walnuts, ⅔ cup mayonnaise and dash pepper. Line 6 pita pocket halves with lettuce leaf; fill with chicken mixture.

Chicken-Tortellini Salad: Toss 1 package (9 ounces) cooked and drained cheese-filled tortellini, 6 cups assorted salad greens, 3 cups cubed cooked chicken and ½ cup creamy Italian or Caesar salad dressing; sprinkle with shredded Parmesan cheese.

Pesto Chicken and Pasta: Toss 4 cups hot cooked pasta with 2 cups shredded cooked chicken, ½ cup basil pesto, ½ cup coarsely chopped roasted red bell pepper and ¼ cup sliced ripe olives.

Thai-Broccoli Chicken Peanut Salad: Mix 4 cups broccoli slaw (from 16 ounce bag) with 2 cups shredded cooked chicken and ⅓ to ½ cup purchased peanut sauce. Sprinkle with dry-roasted peanuts and cilantro leaves.

lemon-basil chicken-pasta salad

Prep Time: 25 Minutes • **Start to Finish:** 1 Hour 25 Minutes • 4 servings

2 cups uncooked rotini or rotelle pasta (6 oz)

10 asparagus spears, trimmed, cut into 1-inch pieces (about 2 cups)

2 cups cubed cooked chicken

1 clove garlic, finely chopped, or ⅛ teaspoon garlic powder

½ cup fresh basil leaves, torn lengthwise into thin strips

½ cup shredded Parmesan cheese (2 oz)

¼ cup olive or vegetable oil

1 tablespoon grated lemon peel

1 Cook and drain pasta as directed on package, adding asparagus during last 2 to 3 minutes of cooking. Rinse with cold water to cool; drain.

2 In large glass or plastic bowl, toss pasta and asparagus with chicken. Stir in garlic, basil, cheese, oil and lemon peel. Cover with plastic wrap; refrigerate 1 to 2 hours or until chilled.

1 Serving: Calories 440; Total Fat 21g (Saturated Fat 5g; Trans Fat 0g); Cholesterol 45mg; Sodium 250mg; Total Carbohydrate 39g (Dietary Fiber 3g); Protein 24g **Exchanges:** 2 Starch, 1 Vegetable, 2½ Lean Meat, 2½ Fat **Carbohydrate Choices:** 2½

a new twist

Try ham instead of chicken and Swiss cheese instead of the Parmesan for a different but delicious flavor change.

ultimate chicken-pasta salad

Prep Time: 30 Minutes • **Start to Finish:** 1 Hour 30 Minutes • 10 servings (1 cup each)

DRESSING

- ⅓ cup milk
- ⅓ cup mayonnaise
- 3 tablespoons sugar
- 3 tablespoons white wine vinegar
- 2 teaspoons poppy seed
- ½ teaspoon salt
- ½ teaspoon celery salt
- ½ teaspoon ground mustard

SALAD

- 1 package (16 oz) gemelli pasta
- 2 cups diced cooked chicken
- 1 cup sweetened dried cherries
- ½ cup sliced celery
- ½ cup slivered almonds, toasted*

1 In small bowl, mix dressing ingredients with whisk until well blended. Cover; refrigerate until ready to use.

2 Cook and drain pasta as directed on package. Rinse with cold water to cool; drain well.

3 In large bowl, mix pasta, chicken, cherries and celery. Mix dressing mixture again with whisk; pour over salad and toss gently to coat. Cover; refrigerate 1 to 2 hours until chilled. Stir in almonds.

*To toast almonds, sprinkle in ungreased skillet. Cook over medium heat 5 to 7 minutes, stirring frequently until nuts begin to brown, then stirring constantly until nuts are light brown.

1 Serving: Calories 410; Total Fat 12g (Saturated Fat 2g; Trans Fat 0g); Cholesterol 25mg; Sodium 290mg; Total Carbohydrate 58g (Dietary Fiber 4g); Protein 18g **Exchanges:** 4 Starch, 1 Lean Meat, 1 Fat **Carbohydrate Choices:** 4

make-ahead

This salad can be made a day ahead; cover and refrigerate. Stir before serving. If needed, add a tablespoon or two of milk to make it more creamy.

chicken-thyme-penne salad

Prep Time: 30 Minutes • **Start to Finish:** 4 Hours 30 Minutes • 12 servings (1 cup each)

3 cups uncooked penne pasta (9 oz)

4 cups cubed deli rotisserie chicken (from 2- to 3-lb chicken)

2 cups seedless red grapes, cut in half

2 medium stalks celery, sliced (1 cup)

⅓ cup chopped onion

3 tablespoons olive or vegetable oil

2 tablespoons chopped fresh or 2 teaspoons dried thyme leaves, crushed

1¼ cups reduced-fat mayonnaise or salad dressing

1 tablespoon milk

1 tablespoon honey

1 tablespoon coarse-grained mustard

1 teaspoon salt

1 cup chopped walnuts, toasted*

1 Cook and drain pasta as directed on package. Rinse with cold water to cool; drain.

2 In very large (4-quart) bowl, mix pasta, chicken, grapes, celery and onion. In small bowl, mix oil and 1 tablespoon of the fresh thyme (or 1 teaspoon of the dried thyme). Pour over chicken mixture; toss to coat.

3 In small bowl, mix mayonnaise, milk, honey, mustard, salt and remaining thyme. Cover salad and dressing separately; refrigerate at least 4 hours but no longer than 24 hours.

4 Up to 2 hours before serving, toss salad with dressing. Cover; refrigerate until serving. Just before serving, stir in ¾ cup of the walnuts. Sprinkle salad with remaining ¼ cup walnuts.

*To toast walnuts, sprinkle in ungreased skillet. Cook over medium heat 5 to 7 minutes, stirring frequently until nuts begin to brown, then stirring constantly until nuts are light brown.

1 Serving: Calories 400; Total Fat 22g (Saturated Fat 3.5g; Trans Fat 0g); |Cholesterol 50mg; Sodium 610mg; Total Carbohydrate 30g (Dietary Fiber 2g); Protein 19g **Exchanges:** 1½ Starch, ½ Other Carbohydrate, 2 Lean Meat, 3 Fat **Carbohydrate Choices:** 2

a new twist

We love to top this easy salad with about ½ cup crumbled blue cheese.

chicken salad sandwiches

Prep Time: 10 Minutes • **Start to Finish:** 10 Minutes • 4 sandwiches

1½ cups chopped cooked chicken or turkey

1 medium stalk celery, chopped (½ cup)

1 small onion, finely chopped (⅓ cup)

½ cup mayonnaise or salad dressing

¼ teaspoon salt

¼ teaspoon pepper

8 slices bread

1 In medium bowl, mix all ingredients except bread.

2 Spread mixture evenly on 4 of the bread slices. Top with remaining bread slices.

1 Sandwich: Calories 430; Total Fat 27g (Saturated Fat 4.5g; Trans Fat 0g); Cholesterol 60mg; Sodium 630mg; Total Carbohydrate 27g (Dietary Fiber 1g); Protein 19g
Exchanges: 2 Starch, 2 Lean Meat, 4 Fat **Carbohydrate Choices:** 2

a new twist

For variety, add some favorite ingredients to the mix in this sandwich mixture. Chopped hard-cooked egg, pickle relish, pimiento or roasted bell pepper or even shredded cheese are all interesting, tasty additions to try.

chicken salad club sandwich stackers

Prep Time: 15 Minutes • **Start to Finish:** 15 Minutes • 4 servings (½ sandwich each)

⅓ cup mayonnaise

1 teaspoon honey mustard

2 cups shredded cooked chicken breast

⅓ cup finely chopped celery

6 slices whole-grain bread, toasted

8 slices tomato

4 slices bacon, cooked, drained and cut in half

4 leaves romaine or leaf lettuce

4 tiny dill or sweet gherkins

1 In medium bowl, mix mayonnaise and mustard. Stir in chicken and celery until well mixed.

2 Spread ½ cup chicken mixture on one side of 2 bread slices. Layer each with 2 tomato slices, 2 half slices of bacon and 1 lettuce leaf. Top each with another bread slice. Repeat layers, starting with chicken mixture. Top each with third bread slice.

3 Thread pickles on toothpicks; insert 2 into each sandwich. Cut each sandwich in half to serve.

1 Serving: Calories 420; Total Fat 22g (Saturated Fat 4.5g; Trans Fat 0g); Cholesterol 75mg; Sodium 620mg; Total Carbohydrate 25g (Dietary Fiber 5g); Protein 29g
Exchanges: 1 Starch, ½ Other Carbohydrate, ½ Vegetable, 3½ Lean Meat, 2 Fat
Carbohydrate Choices: 1½

chicken souvlaki sandwiches

Prep Time: 15 Minutes • **Start to Finish:** 15 Minutes • 6 sandwiches

3 cups chopped
cooked chicken

1 cup chopped
peeled cucumber

½ cup crumbled feta
cheese (2 oz)

⅓ cup finely chopped
red onion

⅓ cup sour cream

2 tablespoons chopped
fresh dill weed

2 tablespoons mayonnaise
or salad dressing

1 tablespoon red
wine vinegar

¼ teaspoon salt

⅛ teaspoon pepper

6 pita fold breads (5 inch),
warmed

1 In medium bowl, place all ingredients except pita breads; toss until evenly coated.

2 Divide chicken mixture evenly down center of each pita bread; fold in half.

1 Sandwich: Calories 340; Total Fat 14g (Saturated Fat 5g; Trans Fat 0g); Cholesterol 80mg; Sodium 690mg; Total Carbohydrate 27g (Dietary Fiber 1g); Protein 26g
Exchanges: 1½ Starch, ½ Vegetable, 3 Lean Meat, 1 Fat **Carbohydrate Choices:** 2

swap it out

Greek yogurt instead of the mayonnaise is a nice substitution and adds a little extra zing to this sandwich.

fast 'n fresh chicken sandwiches

Prep Time: 10 Minutes • **Start to Finish:** 10 Minutes • 4 sandwiches

8 slices rustic raisin-nut or cranberry-nut bread

½ cup mascarpone cheese

4 medium green onions, chopped (¼ cup)

4 teaspoons chopped fresh dill weed

1 package (9 oz) thin-sliced cooked chicken breast

1 On one side of each bread slice, spread 1 tablespoon cheese. On 4 of the bread slices, evenly sprinkle onions. On remaining 4 bread slices, evenly sprinkle dill.

2 Divide chicken among onion-topped bread slices; cover with dill-topped bread slices.

1 Sandwich: Calories 260; Total Fat 4.5g (Saturated Fat 1g; Trans Fat 0.5g); Cholesterol 35mg; Sodium 1000mg; Total Carbohydrate 34g (Dietary Fiber 3g); Protein 20g **Exchanges:** 1½ Starch, 1 Other Carbohydrate, 2 Very Lean Meat, ½ Fat **Carbohydrate Choices:** 2

chicken, vegetable and cream cheese sandwiches

Prep Time: 10 Minutes • **Start to Finish:** 10 Minutes • 4 sandwiches

- 8 slices pumpernickel bread
- 1 container (6.5 oz) garlic-and-herbs spreadable cheese
- 16 thin slices cucumber
- 1 lb sliced cooked chicken (from deli)
- 1 medium tomato, sliced
- 1 slice (¼ inch thick) sweet onion, separated into rings
- 1 cup coleslaw mix (from 16-oz bag)

1 Spread one side of each bread slice with cheese.

2 Top 4 of the bread slices, cheese side up, evenly with cucumber, chicken, tomato, onion and coleslaw mix. Cover with remaining 4 bread slices, cheese side down.

1 Sandwich: Calories 550; Total Fat 26g (Saturated Fat 12g, Trans Fat 0.5g); Cholesterol 150mg; Sodium 740mg; Total Carbohydrate 35g (Dietary Fiber 4g); Protein 43g **Exchanges:** 2 Starch, 1 Vegetable, 5 Very Lean Meat, 4½ Fat **Carbohydrate Choices:** 2

italian chicken club

Prep Time: 15 Minutes • **Start to Finish:** 15 Minutes • 6 sandwiches

6 focaccia or ciabatta rolls, split

½ cup basil pesto

4 teaspoons balsamic vinegar

½ lb thinly sliced oven-roasted chicken breast (from deli)

⅓ cup sun-dried tomatoes in oil, drained, thinly sliced

6 slices mozzarella cheese

1 Cut each focaccia bread in half horizontally. In small bowl, mix pesto and vinegar. Spread mixture on cut side of roll bottoms.

2 Top evenly with chicken, tomatoes and mozzarella. Cover with bread tops.

1 Sandwich: Calories 660; Total Fat 31g (Saturated Fat 7g; Trans Fat 0g); Cholesterol 30mg; Sodium 1920mg; Total Carbohydrate 71g (Dietary Fiber 4g); Protein 23g **Exchanges:** 4½ Starch, 1½ Lean Meat, 4½ Fat **Carbohydrate Choices:** 5

swap it out

Sliced fresh tomatoes can be substituted for the sun-dried tomatoes.

apricot-dijon chicken sandwiches

Prep Time: 10 Minutes ● **Start to Finish:** 10 Minutes ● 4 sandwiches

1 loaf ciabatta bread (12 oz)

¼ cup Dijon mustard

¼ cup apricot preserves

4 leaves Bibb or Boston lettuce

¾ lb thinly sliced deli rotisserie chicken

1 Cut bread in half horizontally. In small bowl, mix mustard and preserves; spread over cut sides of bread.

2 On bread bottom, layer lettuce and chicken. Cover with bread top. Cut lengthwise down center, then cut crosswise in half into 4 sandwiches.

1 Sandwich: Calories 400; Total Fat 9g (Saturated Fat 2g; Trans Fat 0g); Cholesterol 75mg; Sodium 1200mg; Total Carbohydrate 50g (Dietary Fiber 2g); Protein 30g
Exchanges: 3 Starch, ½ Other Carbohydrate, 1 Very Lean Meat, 2 Lean Meat
Carbohydrate Choices: 3

swap it out

Try fig jam in place of the apricot preserves.

country chicken sandwiches with maple-mustard spread

Prep Time: 15 Minutes • **Start to Finish:** 15 Minutes • 4 sandwiches

3 tablespoons mayonnaise or salad dressing

2 tablespoons country-style Dijon mustard

2 tablespoons real maple syrup

1 small shallot, finely chopped (about 3 tablespoons)

8 slices rustic bread

4 slices (1 oz each) Swiss cheese

2 cups sliced deli rotisserie chicken (from 2- to 3-lb chicken)

1 medium ripe avocado, pitted, peeled and sliced

1 In small bowl, mix mayonnaise, mustard, syrup and shallot. Spread on one side of each bread slice.

2 Top 4 slices of bread with cheese, chicken and avocado. Top with remaining bread slices.

1 Sandwich: Calories 460; Total Fat 23g (Saturated Fat 5g; Trans Fat 0.5g); Cholesterol 70mg; Sodium 660mg; Total Carbohydrate 37g (Dietary Fiber 4g); Protein 26g **Exchanges:** 2½ Starch, 2½ Lean Meat, 2½ Fat **Carbohydrate Choices:** 2½

caesar chicken subs

Prep Time: 15 Minutes • **Start to Finish:** 15 Minutes • 4 sandwiches

1 French bread baguette (8 oz)

⅓ cup Caesar dressing

½ package (3.5-oz size) giant sliced pepperoni

¾ lb deli rotisserie chicken, cut into ¼-inch slices

4 slices (1 oz each) Colby–Monterey Jack cheese blend

4 slices tomato, cut in half

4 lettuce leaves

½ medium red onion, thinly sliced

1 Cut bread into fourths, then cut each horizontally in half. Spread dressing over cut sides of bread.

2 On bread bottoms, layer pepperoni, chicken, cheese, tomato, lettuce and onion. Cover with bread tops; press gently. Secure with toothpicks.

1 Sandwich: Calories 620; Total Fat 35g (Saturated Fat 12g; Trans Fat 1g); Cholesterol 120mg; Sodium 1320mg; Total Carbohydrate 36g (Dietary Fiber 2g); Protein 41g
Exchanges: 1½ Starch, ½ Other Carbohydrate, ½ Vegetable, 2 Very Lean Meat, 2 Lean Meat, 1 High-Fat Meat, 4 Fat **Carbohydrate Choices:** 2½

make-ahead

You can make these sandwiches ahead of time, but add the tomato slices just before serving.

thai chicken salad cones

Prep Time: 20 Minutes • **Start to Finish:** 20 Minutes • 4 servings (2 cones each)

DRESSING

- 1 tablespoon packed brown sugar
- 2 tablespoons creamy peanut butter
- 2 tablespoons rice vinegar or cider vinegar
- 1 tablespoon fish sauce
- ⅛ teaspoon ground red pepper (cayenne)

SALAD

- 2 cans (10 oz each) chunk light chicken, drained
- 1½ cups coleslaw mix (from 16-oz bag)
- ½ cup chopped seeded cucumber
- ½ cup chopped fresh cilantro
- ¼ cup coarsely chopped dry-roasted peanuts
- 4 spinach-flavor flour tortillas (8 to 10 inch)

1 In small bowl, mix dressing ingredients with whisk.

2 In medium bowl, mix all salad ingredients except tortillas. Add dressing; toss to coat.

3 Cut each tortilla in half; form each into cone shape. Spoon chicken salad into cones.

1 Serving: Calories 370; Total Fat 14g (Saturated Fat 3g; Trans Fat 0.5g); Cholesterol 50mg; Sodium 1150mg; Total Carbohydrate 34g (Dietary Fiber 3g); Protein 26g
Exchanges: 1½ Starch, ½ Other Carbohydrate, ½ Vegetable, 3 Very Lean Meat, 2½ Fat
Carbohydrate Choices: 2

swap it out

Soy sauce can be substituted for fish sauce, and regular flour tortillas can be used instead of spinach-flavor tortillas.

chicken fajita salad wraps

Prep Time: 30 Minutes • **Start to Finish:** 30 Minutes • 8 servings

DRESSING

- 1 **cup ranch dressing**
- 1 **tablespoon lime juice**
- 1 **tablespoon finely chopped chipotle chiles in adobo sauce (from 7-oz can)**
- 1 **teaspoon grated lime peel**

WRAPS

- 3 **cups chopped deli rotisserie chicken (from 2- to 3-lb chicken)**
- 2 **cups thinly sliced iceberg lettuce**
- 1 **cup frozen corn (from 12-oz bag), cooked, cooled**
- 1 **small tomato, seeded, chopped (⅓ cup)**
- 1 **cup shredded Monterey Jack cheese (4 oz)**
- 1 **package (11 oz) flour tortillas for burritos (8 tortillas; 8 inch)**

  Chunky-style salsa, if desired

  Sour cream, if desired

1 In small bowl, mix dressing ingredients; set aside. In large bowl, stir together chicken, lettuce, corn and tomato. Add dressing; toss to coat.

2 Spoon chicken mixture evenly down center of each tortilla; sprinkle with cheese. Roll up. Serve immediately with salsa and sour cream.

1 Serving: Calories 420; Total Fat 26g (Saturated Fat 7g; Trans Fat 1g); Cholesterol 50mg; Sodium 1360mg; Total Carbohydrate 30g (Dietary Fiber 2g); Protein 17g **Exchanges:** 2 Starch, 1½ Medium-Fat Meat, 3 Fat **Carbohydrate Choices:** 2

chicken salad roll-ups

Prep Time: 30 Minutes • **Start to Finish:** 1 Hour 30 Minutes • 24 servings

2 cups chopped cooked chicken

3 medium green onions, chopped (3 tablespoons)

¼ cup chopped walnuts

½ cup creamy poppy seed dressing

½ cup cream cheese spread (from 8-oz container)

2 flour tortillas (10 inch)

6 leaves Bibb lettuce

½ cup finely chopped fresh strawberries

1 In food processor, place chicken, onions and walnuts. Cover; process, using quick on-and-off motions, until finely chopped. Add ⅓ cup of the poppy seed dressing. Cover; process just until mixed. In small bowl, mix remaining dressing and the cream cheese spread with spoon until smooth.

2 Spread cream cheese mixture evenly over entire surface of tortillas. Remove white rib from lettuce leaves. Press lettuce into cream cheese mixture, tearing to fit and leaving top 2 inches of tortillas uncovered. Spread chicken mixture over lettuce; top with strawberries.

3 Firmly roll up tortillas, beginning at bottom. Wrap each roll in plastic wrap. Refrigerate at least 1 hour. Trim ends of each roll. With sharp serrated knife, cut rolls into ½- to ¾-inch slices.

1 Serving: Calories 70; Total Fat 4g (Saturated Fat 1.5g; Trans Fat 0g); Cholesterol 20mg; Sodium 50mg; Total Carbohydrate 5g (Dietary Fiber 0g); Protein 4g **Exchanges:** ½ High-Fat Meat, ½ Fat **Carbohydrate Choices:** ½

swap it out

If you can't find creamy poppy seed dressing, you can use coleslaw dressing, regular or low-fat mayonnaise or salad dressing instead.

Metric Conversion Guide

VOLUME

U.S. Units	Canadian Metric	Australian Metric
¼ teaspoon	1 mL	1 ml
½ teaspoon	2 mL	2 ml
1 teaspoon	5 mL	5 ml
1 tablespoon	15 mL	20 ml
¼ cup	50 mL	60 ml
⅓ cup	75 mL	80 ml
½ cup	125 mL	125 ml
⅔ cup	150 mL	170 ml
¾ cup	175 mL	190 ml
1 cup	250 mL	250 ml
1 quart	1 liter	1 liter
1½ quarts	1.5 liters	1.5 liters
2 quarts	2 liters	2 liters
2½ quarts	2.5 liters	2.5 liters
3 quarts	3 liters	3 liters
4 quarts	4 liters	4 liters

WEIGHT

U.S. Units	Canadian Metric	Australian Metric
1 ounce	30 grams	30 grams
2 ounces	55 grams	60 grams
3 ounces	85 grams	90 grams
4 ounces (¼ pound)	115 grams	125 grams
8 ounces (½ pound)	225 grams	225 grams
16 ounces (1 pound)	455 grams	500 grams
1 pound	455 grams	0.5 kilogram

MEASUREMENTS

Inches	Centimeters
1	2.5
2	5.0
3	7.5
4	10.0
5	12.5
6	15.0
7	17.5
8	20.5
9	23.0
10	25.5
11	28.0
12	30.5
13	33.0

TEMPERATURES

Fahrenheit	Celsius
32°	0°
212°	100°
250°	120°
275°	140°
300°	150°
325°	160°
350°	180°
375°	190°
400°	200°
425°	220°
450°	230°
475°	240°
500°	260°

Note: The recipes in this cookbook have not been developed or tested using metric measures. When converting recipes to metric, some variations in quality may be noted.

index

Recipe Testing and Calculating Nutrition Information

Recipe Testing:

- Large eggs and 2% milk were used unless otherwise indicated.

- Fat-free, low-fat, low-sodium or lite products were not used unless indicated.

- No nonstick cookware and bakeware were used unless otherwise indicated. No dark-colored, black or insulated bakeware was used.

- When a pan is specified, a metal pan was used; a baking dish or pie plate means ovenproof glass was used.

- An electric hand mixer was used for mixing only when mixer speeds are specified.

Calculating Nutrition:

- The first ingredient was used wherever a choice is given, such as ⅓ cup sour cream or plain yogurt.

- The first amount was used wherever a range is given, such as 3- to 3 ½-pound whole chicken.

- The first serving number was used wherever a range is given, such as 4 to 6 servings.

- "If desired" ingredients were not included.

- Only the amount of a marinade or frying oil that is absorbed was included.